RAILBIKE

Cycling On Abandoned Railroads

by Bob Mellin

Balboa Publishing

San Anselmo, CA

The development of this book was based on the experience and knowledge of the author with input from the numerous resources noted in the acknowledgements, text, appendix and bibliography. The information contained herein is true and complete to the best of the author's knowledge and is not intended to promote the violation of any laws or statutes.

The author and publisher disclaim any and all liability incurred because of the use of information contained in this book.

Wholesale rates available to Railroad and Cycling organizations, Government Agencies and the trade.

© 1996, Robert A. Mellin, Jr.

First Edition

10 9 8 7 6 5 4 3 2 1

Printed in the United States of America

Library of Congress
Cataloging in Publication Data
Mellin, Robert A., Jr.

RAILBIKE — Cycling on Abandoned Railroads

Library of Congress Catalog Card No.: 95-094676
ISBN 0-935902-29-5 Paperback

Front Cover Photograph by Dr. Richard Smart
   "**Crossing a Washout**"
   Richard Smart's long-time Railcycling companion
   Ken Wright on 250 mile Wilderness Railcycle ride
   in 1987. Near Bear Lake in Northern British Columbia.

Photography by Bob Mellin except where otherwise credited.

Back Cover Photograph: Bob, Haley and Joe Mellin (left to right)

Computer Graphics: Trevor Ferruggia

Published by:

Balboa Publishing
1323 San Anselmo Ave
San Anselmo
California 94960

E-Mail: **BALBOAPUB @ AOL . COM**

TABLE OF CONTENTS

To Joe & Haley

ACKNOWLEDGEMENTS

The author appreciates the support and information provided by:

William J. Gillum, inventor, railbike designer and founder of the American Railbike Association. Mr. Gillum was the first modern-day railbiker to draw national media attention to riding the rails.

Mrs. Lyllian Mary Gillum, for sharing her treasured photographs and clippings of her late husband and his railbike work.

Dr. Richard Smart, creator of the term "Railcycle" and inventor of the patented Railcycle, the first practical railbike which may be ridden on rails or roads.

Waldo J. Nielsen, author of "Right of Way - A Guide to Abandoned Railroads in the United States."

Ron Forster, designer of railbike adaptations for the blind and handicapped; successor to Mr. Gillum at his death in continuing the American Railbike Association.

Joseph and Haley Mellin, photograph models, railbike passengers, and enduring audience for countless railbike tales.

Sharon L. Nielsen, consistent source of encouragement and tireless proofreader.

International Human Powered Vehicle Association (IHPVA), for continued support of railbike research and development.

"Riding the rails on a bike
is a rewarding and remarkably pleasant experience."

William J. Gillum
{ 1923 ~ 1980 }

GETTING STARTED

I built my first railbike over 25 years ago.

It was a simple, four-wheeled platform with a bicycle mounted in the middle and a passenger seat on each side. I talked my brother, Jim, and my dad into coming along for the maiden voyage.

We assembled the railbike one spring morning on abandoned tracks near my home in California, about a mile from San Quentin prison. With very little fanfare, we climbed aboard and away we went.

I sat in the middle and pedaled while my family relaxed and enjoyed the view. I was using a single-speed cruiser bicycle and quickly realized that the gear ratio was a problem.

Though I pedaled feverishly, the railbike was moving more slowly than I had hoped. Next time, I thought, I'd use a three-speed bike.

But regardless of the speed, the railbike worked! I was delighted that there were no major design flaws and

Bob Mellin, father, author, railbike pedaler.

we glided down the tracks, over a trestle bridging a San Francisco Bay inlet, and on our way to adventure.

But within minutes, my passengers commented on our rather conservative top speed - about 8 m.p.h. I explained

that the only gears I could find at the junk yard didn't allow gearing up from the bicycle to the drive axle. Unimpressed, my brother observed that it was getting late, and my father noticed the day was especially "warm out here on the railbed."

Armed with this encouragement, I turned us around, pedaled back to our starting point, and packed up my invention. A few months later, when I joined the Army, my railbike ended up in a dumpster.

Over the years I continued my interest in railbiking, though other things (job, kids, etc.) took precedence. I saw the railbike article in the February 1976 issue of Popular Mechanics and mailed away for more information. For $10 I got a membership in the American Railbike Association and an informative handbook telling a lot of things about railbikes.

I live in the small community I grew up in. Coincidentally, it's the same community that gave birth to the now ubiquitous mountain bike. Hundreds of cyclists traverse the bike path in front of my home each day. Although most of these riders are

This Popular Mechanics articled drew national attention.

going somewhere with a purpose, many are simply riding for the joy of riding.

It occurred to me that some of these cyclists might enjoy the same railbiking experiences that I enjoy. So I decided to share my experiences by writing a book about railbiking.

I looked forward to building some working railbikes and reliving my youthful railbike experiences with my children. I remembered the joy of my first railbike trip. I hoped to share this experience with family, friends and book customers.

But I knew that the key to sharing my railbike interest is sharing access to usable rails. I thought of a book called "Right-Of-Way" which I got with my American Railbike Association membership 20 years ago. It identified almost 35,000 miles of abandoned tracks in the United States. Though the author had died and the publisher (Old Bottle Magazine) was no longer listed, I was able to locate a distributor of the book in Bend, Oregon.

I was delighted to learn that not only was the book still available, but that it had been revised recently to

On my trip to Bend, Oregon, I was happy to find conference facilities available for my important meetings.

include an additional 50,000 miles of abandoned track. I visited Ken and Shirley Asher of Maverick Distributors in Bend to discuss making the revised "Right-Of-Way" guide available to railbikers. I also visited their son Ken, who, with author Waldo Nielsen, published the revised edition, through his company, Maverick Publications.

Though their storefront presence can best be described as modest, the Asher's distribution operation handles an impressive number of titles, some even more obscure than "Right-Of-Way." After a comprehensive tour of the Maverick facilities, I thanked the Ashers for their hospitality and returned to writing my "RAILBIKE" book. I felt encouraged that with more than 80,000 miles of abandoned track to explore, my audience would now be able to do more than just read about railbiking.

Maverick Distributors' modest storefront belies its impressive inventory of eclectic publications.

"RAILBIKE - Cycling On Abandoned Railroads" is intended to provide an overview of the history of the railbike and a feel for what the railbiking experience is about. To share a sense of the experience of riding the rails, I've included interviews with several railbike "activists" who share my obsession with this special method of transportation.

Railbikes have been around for over 100 years and dozens, if not hundreds, of different designs have been used. By exploring the history of the railbike, you may gain an appreciation for the skill and ingenuity employed by the many tinkerers and inventors who have built their ideas into ever-evolving railbike designs.

The nature of railbiking makes it more than the average thrill-sport or mode of exercise. It combines the special benefits of cycling with the opportunity to explore open space few people ever see. And all of this happens on the inescapably massive foundation of the rail lines, which injects the railrider with a sense of respect for the history of the path he has chosen.

I hope that this book conveys some of the heritage, the challenge, the danger, and the joy of railbiking.

My son Joe rides the rails.

RAILBIKE SAFETY

This chapter is put at the beginning of the book because it is VERY IMPORTANT. It's a real good idea to read it and remember what is said if you are thinking of railbiking.

As with most recreational activities, railbiking involves a certain amount of risk. This risk typically falls into two categories:

1. the consequences of trespassing,

2. physical injury.

Though the consequences of getting caught trespassing are not as severe as personal injury, they are most unpleasant nonetheless. <u>Avoid trespassing at all costs!</u>

Obviously, all active rail lines are off-limits. But even those that appear abandoned may technically be "active" and even if they are never used they may be private property. Just because there are no signs saying "No Trespassing" doesn't mean you are welcome to use the tracks.

How are you going to get caught?

Whether abandoned or not, tracks with "No Trespassing" signs are off-limits to railbikers without permission.

There are lots of ways.

Most often, local police are aware that rail lines are privately owned and are instructed to enforce no trespassing laws. Anyone observing you riding the rails can call the local police and then you have a problem.

There also exists a special group called "Railroad Police" who patrol the tracks in special rail vehicles for the expressed purpose of protecting the integrity of the tracks and catching trespassers. As you might imagine, the Railroad Police are not big railbike fans. You can anticipate suffering the most dire consequences if you are caught trespassing by this arm of the law.

Hey, with 80,000 miles of legally abandoned rails in the United States alone to choose from, why risk it?

The other risk railbikers run is physical injury. As some of the railbike enthusiasts describe later in this book, the

If you don't believe railroad police exist,

who do you think rides in these?

Railbiking isn't kid stuff. Safety is important.

Photo courtesy of Paul Morningstar

effects of a crash or derailment can be painful. And that's not counting mishaps involving being hit by a train.

And trains are not the only motorized vehicles using the tracks. Railroad maintenance and inspection crews drive regular cars and trucks fitted with small rail wheels, sometimes at high speeds. Because these vehicles ride on rubber tires, they are very quiet and can approach very fast. Don't assume you will hear them coming!

Yet railbiking can be safe, legal and enjoyable. In the interest of objectivity, I will attempt to present both sides of the railbike safety argument, so readers will be aware of the issues from both points of view.

The argument against railbiking was offered in the form of a January 23, 1986 CONSUMER ALERT issued by the Association of American Railroads addressed to reporters and editors:

CYCLE FOR RIDING RAILS ENDANGERS CONSUMERS

If someone suggests that you do a story about an imaginative contraption for cycling on railroad tracks . . . **BEWARE.**

Individuals marketing such devices seldom, if ever, mention the life-threatening dangers associated with their use or that unauthorized use of them on railroad tracks — active or abandoned — is illegal.

The facts are these:

Railroad tracks — even abandoned — are private property and trespassing is illegal. Rights-of-way no longer needed for rail traffic sometimes are sold to state or local authorities for recreational purposes such as hiking, biking, or equestrian trails. In those cases the rails would be removed. If the rails are still in place, it is likely that the property is still owned by the railroad and may, in fact, still be in use. Moreover, track where a train has not recently run is not necessarily an abandoned track.

In some agricultural areas tracks are used only seasonally — but are subject to use at any time.

But even if one were fortunate enough not to meet a train while pedalling along the track, there are other safety considerations.

Some of the so-called "rail" bikes are very unstable, and spills are common. Falling off of a conventional bicycle traveling on a roadway or bike path is bad enough; falling off a cycle onto a roadbed of wooden crossties, gravel ballast, and steel rails — usually in an isolated location — is courting very serious injury.

Rights-of-way which are no longer used for rail traffic are, obviously, not maintained. Therefore, a cyclist may well encounter broken rails, washouts, rock slides, or other debris, and even deteriorating or collapsed bridges and tunnels.

Cyclists might also encounter motor vehicles at highway crossings. Certainly even the most cautious motorist, alert to the possible approach of trains, would not expect to find a cyclist in the crossing.

It should also be remembered that abandoned spur lines are often connected to heavily traveled mainline track. Therefore a cyclist might easily move from one to the other without realizing it.

And, of course, there is the very real possibility that buyers of cycles, finding there is no unused trackage in their area, will simply take their vehicle out onto the nearest rail line — erroneously assuming that they will have ample time to get off the track if a train approaches. The obvious appeal for children to engage in such activity is especially frightening, and one type of "rail" bike actually is being promoted for use by handicapped persons!

The potential for accidental death or injury on the rails is real. According to the Federal Railroad Administration, some 588 trespassers were killed on railroad rights-of-way in 1984, and 773 others were injured. Those injuries included 161 amputations. Victims included 114 children who were playing on railroad tracks. If bike riders are lured to the rails, those numbers undoubtedly would grow. Trains tend to move much more swiftly and more quietly than

people expect them to, and, as these sad statistics demonstrate, getting out of the way is easier said than done.

So, if you are approached to do a story about "rail" bikes, we hope you will consider these facts first — and reject promoting activity which can be both dangerous and illegal.

The other side of the railbike safety argument was prepared by a railbike proponent who has a different opinion:

I would like to address a consumer alert that was sent from the Association of American Railroads to reporters and editors throughout the country regarding railbikes.

The alert stated that there were life-threatening dangers associated with railbike use and that their unauthorized use was illegal. This next spring, I will celebrate my 20 year anniversary as a railbiker. I have ridden thousands of miles on the rails.

During this period, I never once felt that my life was endangered. In fact, my feelings were the opposite. It's not until I get to a railroad, fold out the railroad apparatus, and ride silently into the distance that I feel safe.

My railbike operates well as an ordinary mountain bicycle. To get to the tracks, I must ride highways, streets, and country roads like everyone else. I compete with cars, vans, and wide trucks for that slim perimeter of roadway that is sometimes available to bicyclists.

More than once in my travels I have been in a "life threatening" situation trying to make it to the tracks. Twenty years ago I designed my own railbike to get away from automobiles and congestion. I felt then as I feel now that unless there are bicycle paths available, bicycles are more compatible with abandoned railroad tracks than with busy roads.

Some of the advantages that railbiking offers over conventional biking are the following:

1. The grades are almost always very gentle (under 3%).

2. The ride is glassy smooth and very quiet.

3. The rider's hands are often free to take pictures, or eat a sandwich as he or she rides along.

4. The ride is more aesthetically pleasing. The more plant life that grows between the rails, the more interesting the path becomes. Some of my most enjoyable rides have been along rusty rails that lay barely visible in the grass ahead of me. Wildlife is frequently abundant.

5. There is more adventure. I am able to go someplace different and leave behind motorized traffic. As I ride silently along in the countryside, through tunnels and over bridges, I enjoy sights, sounds and smells that are not normally experienced along a highway.

If abandoned tracks were set aside to be used only for railbikes, a great assortment of gear could be stored on the outrigger. I have gone on two 100-mile treks through the wilderness living off of canned goods. I tell my friends that the weight of the food and gear that I take on the rails

is somewhere between bicycle touring and horse packing.

I am not the kind of person who deliberately trespasses for the thrill of breaking the law. I pick up litter along the track and I keep watch for trespassers who may vandalize railroad property. If I saw a problem such as a broken rail I would call the railroad company.

Trespassing on railroad property is not a cut and dried issue. Some tracks are in the middle of streets. Others pass through public parks. People use some railroad lands for recreation like fishing, jogging, hiking, hunting and horseback riding.

Our first railcycles were unstable and spills were common. The new bikes with their improved guidance systems have made a big difference. Falls are now infrequent and further improvements will continue.

As for the cyclist who may unknowingly ride from an abandoned spur onto the busy mainline . . . give the railbiker some credit. Abandoned tracks are weedy and rusty. Mainline tracks have a very vital look to them.

Under the right conditions, it is fine for children to use railbikes. When they are accompanied by adults it is much the same as when children are touring with their parents on conventional bicycles.

If a special closed section of abandoned track was set aside for railbike use and had no highway crossings or other hazards, then this could be an ideal place for children and handicapped persons to ride, especially the blind.

It is our dream that bicyclists from all over the country will play a role in trying to save some of the diminishing miles of abandoned tracks. Hundreds of miles of track are being torn up every month. A railroad track could be used as a railbike pathway for many years with little or no maintenance.

Railbiking is environmentally perfect. Not even tire prints are left behind! A railbike was once easily purchased through the Sears Roebuck catalog. At least two dozen railbikes were patented at the turn of the century. In researching the sport, no history of problems were found.

There is a need for this sport to return, but it will take thousands of supporters to make it happen. Please write to the American Association of Railroads to voice your opinions. Railbikers could help the railroads establish a more positive image that would be good for everyone.

As with most arguments like this, the answer probably lies somewhere in between. Railbikers love their sport and claim they will take the precautions necessary to be safe and respect railroad property. The railroads, understandably, feel they have nothing to gain from the growth of the sport of railbiking, and wish the whole idea would disappear.

History has shown us that situations like this resolve over time as a middle ground is found. There is a precedent for permission to use the rails: private citizens who own their own "Speeders" (miniature rail vehicles

Although there are more than 80,000 miles of abandoned tracks in the U.S., signs like these are hard to find.

like the railroad police use) have for years received permission to use railroads, usually by getting organized into Speeder Clubs and getting liability insurance.

One example of cooperation between a railroad and railcyclists is the cooperative relationship at Tillamook, Oregon. The Port of Tillamook Bay, which owns and operates the 100-plus mile line running from the coast inland toward Portland, has shared the rails with Speeders and railbikers alike. Such use has been pre-scheduled and riders sign the GENERAL RELEASE (liability waiver) which appears on the following page, but access to the rails is available nonetheless.

This waiver might serve as a model for other railroads since the waiver has been tested and has held up through appeals in Federal Court - including the U.S. Supreme Court, according to the Port of Tillamook Bay's Chief Clerk.

It would seem that some arrangement like that in Tillamook could be copied at the hundreds of abandoned railroad sites across the country.

In the interim, remember one thing – **railbiking, like horseback riding or skydiving, can be safe and fun if done correctly, or can be dangerous and a bad idea if done illegally or carelessly.**

———— o ————

GENERAL RELEASE

In consideration of the Port of Tillamook Bay (POTB) granting the undersigned the permission to enter upon and use its railroad property in the vicinity of _____ on the date(s) of _____, and particularly for the purpose of _____, the undersigned, well knowing and appreciating the risk and danger assumed by him/her and that the POTB is under no duty or obligation to grant such permission, hereby assumes all risk and waives any claim arising from any injury to him/her (including death) or loss or damage to his/her property occurring while or resulting from being on or about the POTB railroad right-of-way, premises, structures, motive power or rolling stock, due in whole or in part to the acts or omissions, negligent or otherwise, of the officers, agents, servants, licensees or invitees of the POTB; and the undersigned for himself/herself, his/her executor or administrator assigns and his/her heirs at law and next of kin, hereby releases and forever discharges the POTB, its employees, directors, officers, agents, successors and assigns, and additionally the Oregon Tillamook Railroad Authority(OTRA), its officers and members, for injury to him/her (including death) and loss and damage to his/her property occurring or arising while or resulting from being upon or about said right-of-way, premises, structures, motive power or rolling stock of the POTB, whether due in whole or in part to the condition or operation, negligent or otherwise, of said right-of-way, premises, structures, motive power or rolling stock or in whole or part to the acts or omissions, negligent or otherwise or the officers, agents, licensees or invitees of the POTB or OTRA.

INDEMNITY AGREEMENT. I hereby unconditionally agree to indemnify POTB and OTRA, their officers, directors, employees, agents, and members against any and all liability, loss, costs, damages, fees of attorneys, loss of funds advanced and other expenses which the undersigned may sustain or incur in consequence of the undersigned and/or his/her family and friends from the use of the above railroad property, including, but not limited to, sums paid in respect of liabilities incurred to third parties and in settlement of and expenses paid or incurred in connection with claims, suits or judgments resulting from the undersigned's use of POTB property as aforesaid.

I am 18 years of age or older and have read this general release and indemnity agreement carefully, and I understand that I am assuming for myself and for all minor children accompanying me, all risks of every kind as herein above set forth in this general release and indemnity agreement.

Date: _____ Name: Signed _____ Printed _____

Date: _____ Name: Signed _____ Printed _____

Date: _____ Name: Signed _____ Printed _____

Date: _____ Name: Signed _____ Printed _____

Minor children (less than 18 years of age)

Date _____ Child's Name: Printed _____ Age _____

Date _____ Child's Name: Printed _____ Age _____

Date _____ Child's Name: Printed _____ Age _____

Date _____ Child's Name: Printed _____ Age _____

Adult assuming Above Responsibility for Minor(s): (Must also sign below)

Date: _____ Name: Signed _____ Printed _____

HISTORY OF THE RAILBIKE

As you might expect, the railbike was born out of need rather than as a form of recreation. In the 1800's, workers on and around rail lines needed an inexpensive human powered vehicle by which to travel on the tracks to perform various tasks.

Telegraph workers followed the tracks to install and service their wires, which were strung along side the railroads. Similarly, railroad workers needed a means to travel on the tracks without firing up a locomotive.

To fill this need, a number of vehicles were designed or adapted. These included regular trucks and automobiles fitted with railroad wheels instead of the normal wheels and rubber tires. Special small cars were developed which work crews would kick along the rails. The familiar handcar, a vehicle propelled by pumping up and down on a set of levered handles was also developed for this purpose.

The familiar handcar was durable and widely used, but was too heavy to be considered portable.

But these, as well as other rail-modified vehicles, were heavy, relatively expensive, and difficult to move on and off of the tracks.

Some give credit for inventing a pedal powered rail vehicle to a mechanic from Michigan named George Sheffield, in the late 1800's. He lived about seven miles from his job and a rail line ran conveniently along his commute route. He built a simple three-wheeler he would pedal on the rails between home and work.

One evening he discovered a break in the track on his way home and he stopped a freight train and avoided an accident. The Michigan Central Railroad considered prosecuting George for trespassing but decided to reward him instead.

Sheffield used his new-found celebrity status to promote his new business selling railbikes. Years earlier, two inventors named Perry and Aspinwall patented a device for converting a bicycle into a three-wheeled

This advertisement in the 1980's promoted the tricycle car offered by George S. Sheffield & Company.

railbike. Sheffield eventually bought their patents.

So the common bicycle was adapted to rail travel to provide an inexpensive, lightweight and truly portable means of rail travel. **The railbike was born.**

Railbikes were used by railroad companies to inspect tracks and telegraph lines. The Kansas Pacific Railroad monitored its track on the windy Great Plains by mounting a sail on its railbikes to provide effortless cruising. Railbikes were also carried on board many trains for various uses by railroad employees or, in the event of a breakdown, so someone could ride for help.

Limited use of railbikes by the general public has also been documented. An example is the Kentucky family doctor in the early 1900's described in Bobbie Ann Mason's "Feather Crowns" who visited his patients on "one of them railroad tricycles."

Several companies manufactured railbikes in the early 1900's. The 1908 Sears & Roebuck Catalog offered the "Harris 20th Century Railroad

Attachment" for $5.45. The advertisement explained that "**this transforms the ordinary bicycle into the most practical and durable device for obtaining high speed on railroad tracks, making a regular railroad velocipede out of an ordinary bicycle. It consists of three braces made of seamless steel tubing, telescoped into each other for convenience in adjusting or carrying. They are attached to a steel wheel with double flanges and rubber covered surface, which makes it absolutely noiseless in operation. It is light, strong and simple, and can be attached to or detached from the bicycle in a very few moments. Either a low or a very high rate of speed can be easily maintained, and it is impossible to slip, owing to the rubber tires.**"

The advertisement continued, "**Our illustration plainly indicates the manner of attaching, and when not needed it can be very easily carried on the handle bars, as it takes but a very small amount of space. The parts are substantially made and intended to have great durability. Nicely enameled in black. Weight, 4 pounds. This attachment has become very popular with railroad and telegraph employes, both male and female. No. 19K1639.**"

HARRIS 20TH CENTURY RAILROAD ATTACHMENT

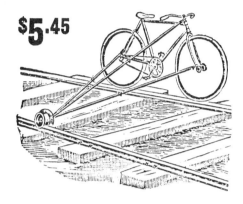

$5.45

The 1908 Sears catalog included this advertisement.

The advertisement went on to offer another option, the "Harris No. 2 Flyer Attachment" for $7.70, which was the "**same as above, with extra wheels to be placed in front and behind bicycle. Especially constructed for persons desiring to secure a high rate of speed, as it will hold the curves better, and sustain heavier loads than the No.1. Weight, 11 pounds. No. 19K1640.**"

Patent drawings for various railbike designs date all the way back to the late 1800's. And over the years each variation has had its own advantages and drawbacks. Some were more stable, but less portable. Some were less expensive but also less durable.

When first introduced, railbikes did not gain widespread acceptance for a number of reasons. The biggest single roadblock to popularity was the fact that 90 years ago the railroads were very active. And sharing the rails with a train is a bad idea. But times have changed, and railbiking opportunities increase every day.

Over the years other modes of transportation have largely replaced the trains. Highways now crisscross the nation and railroad company mergers and economic constraints have led to the abandonment of duplicate or infrequently used rail lines.

In 1916 over 1200 different railroads operated on more than 250,000 miles of track. By 1977 the number of railroad companies had shrunk to 320 with only 168,000 miles of track owned in 1981 (Moody's Transportation Manual, 1986, for all classes of railroads). Today, less than half of our original rail system remains, and an additional 2,000 miles of track are abandoned every year (Rails to Trails Conservancy, Washington, D.C.).

In 1976 railbiking received extensive national media exposure when the February issue of Popular Mechanics included a photograph of William Gillum (see "Railbikers" chapter) riding his self-designed, outrigger-style railbike. Mr. Gillum had done his homework and had amassed a wealth of information including alternative designs, patent drawings for various kinds of railbikes, and the location of abandoned railroads accessible to railbikers.

Initially, Mr. Gillum had thought his design was a new invention. His subsequent patent search revealed that about the turn of the century, dozens of railbike patents had been issued. "Some of these inventions are marvels of engineering and some of them are simple, with graceful lines and few parts. All are fascinating bicycle history," Gillum stated.

William Gillum's railbiking photo in Popular Mechanics generated thousands of inquiries. In response, Mr. Gillum formed the American Railbike Association to serve as a clearing house for railbike information. He provided photographs showing details of construction of his railbike and included

patent drawings of what other inventors had done. He offered these photos and patent drawings and a lifetime membership in the Association for $10.00. Many inventors, tinkerers, bicyclists and railbikers responded.

Mr. Gillum wanted the American Railbike Association to be a means for railbike enthusiasts to exchange information which would facilitate the

Members could hang their certificate anywhere.

growth and development of railbiking across the country. Gillum invited America to "build yourself a railbike. It's easy. And get out and see some pretty country that few people have seen except from a train window."

In 1976, interest seemed high and growth was promising. But the enthusiasm Gillum's media exposure generated gradually subsided and railbiking returned to a state of dormancy during the late 1970's and '80's.

But railbiking is alive, not just in the United States, but in other countries as well. Railbikers interviewed in this book include residents of Canada, Hong Kong and France. A 1986 Miramax film on home video entitled "The Quest" featured the adventures of a young do-it-yourselfer in Australia who was "always looking for a challenge or a new way to do things." The film opens with the hero racing against time on his home made, you guessed it, railbike. As it turns out, this youngster actually got his railbike from Railcycle inventor Richard Smart (see "Railbikers" chapter).

And in the last ten years, as increasing attention has been focused on alternative modes of transportation, organizations such as the International Human Powered Vehicle Association (IHPVA) have supported continued interest in the design and development of railbikes. At its annual European Human Powered Vehicle Championships in Switzerland, the IHPVA sponsored time trials for several contemporary rail vehicles. This type of support provides an invaluable forum for the continued evolution of railbiking.

Everyone should join the IHPVA.

To provide a feel for where that evolutionary process began, the following pages offer a glimpse at some of the early railbike designs and patents:

KAEMPFER'S RAILWAY VELOCIPEDE

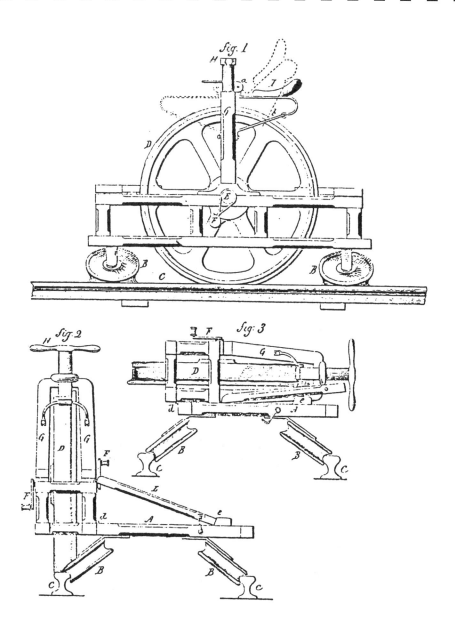

W.H. FOX, PATENT NO. 225,585, MARCH 16, 1880

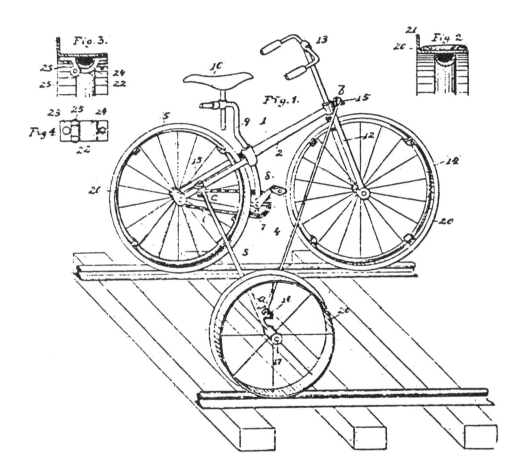

Fig. 3.

Fig. 2

Fig. 4

Fig. 1.

F. BRADY, PATENT NO. 427,663, MAY 13, 1890

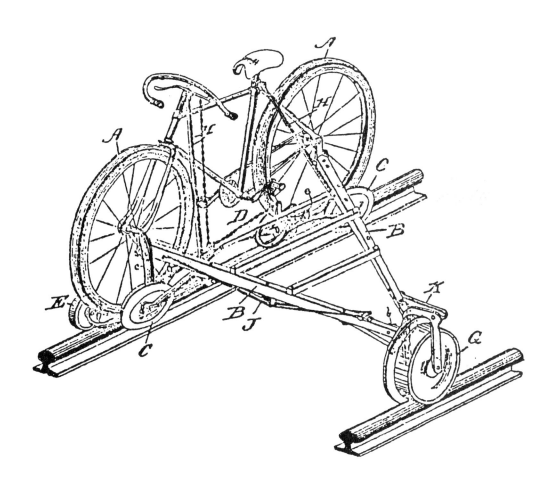

L.J. PARKER, PATENT NO. 551,834, DECEMBER 24, 1895

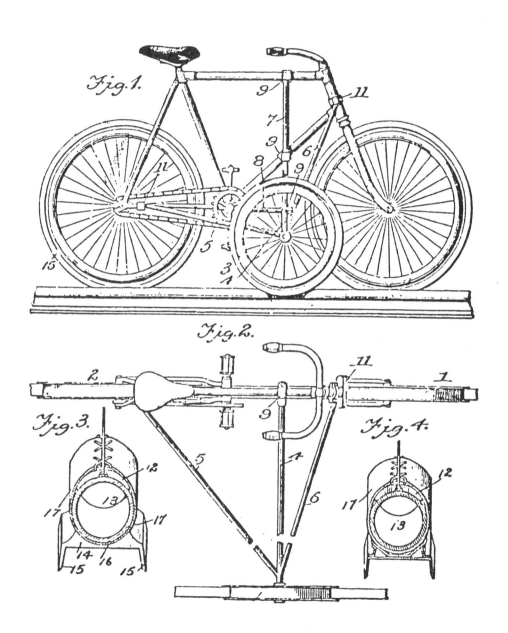

Fig.1.

Fig.2.

Fig.3.

Fig.4.

W.P. BRODERICK, PATENT NO. 588,551, AUGUST 24, 1897

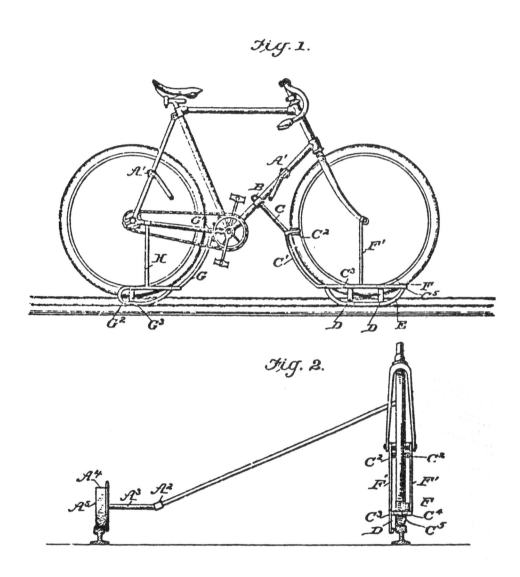

Fig. 1.

Fig. 2.

—— H.J. OTTO & A.E. WIELSCH, PATENT NO. 608,071, JULY 26, 1898 ——

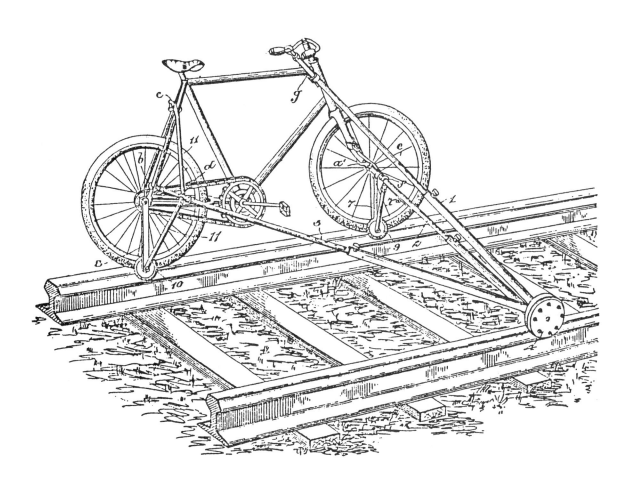

C. GORNEMAN, PATENT NO. 693,128, FEBRUARY 11, 1902

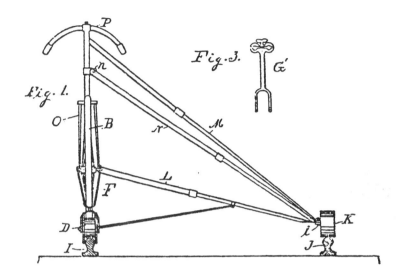

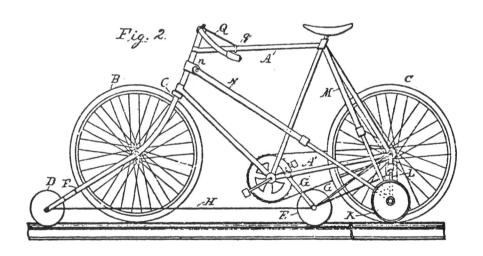

F. GOOCH, PATENT NO. 705,664, JULY 29, 1902

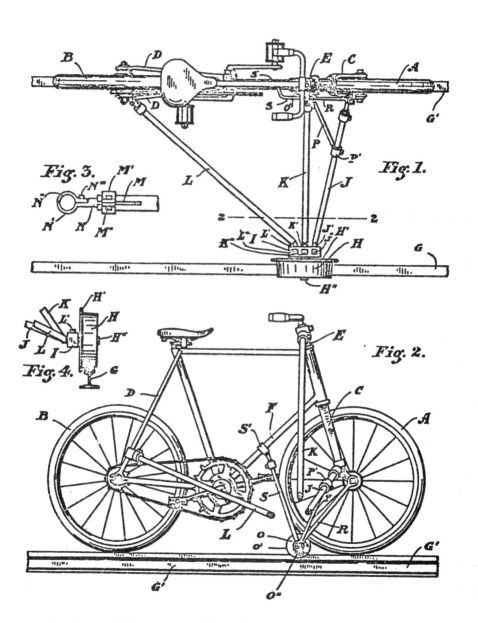

Fig. 3.

Fig. 1.

Fig. 4.

Fig. 2.

W.E. STOCKTON, PATENT NO. 727,708, MAY 12, 1903

Bicycle Railroad - Derailments were painful but infrequent.

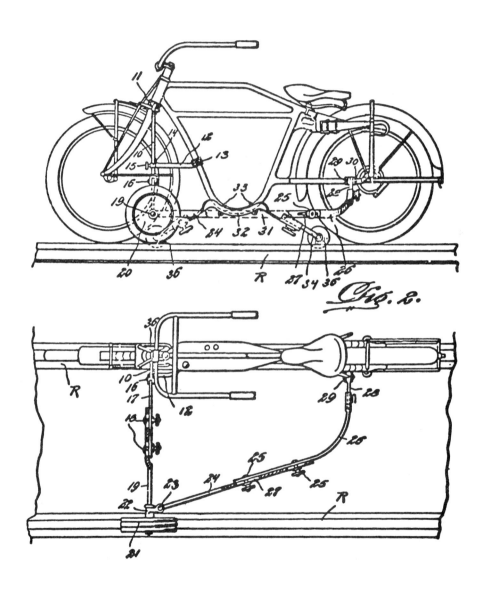

A. REVNY, PATENT NO. 1,436,532, NOVEMBER 21, 1922

1894 - Charles Newton Teetor's Bicycle Car featured thin sheet metal and wire spoke wheels covered with rubber treads to improve traction and to quiet the ride. The double seat model only weighed 75 pounds.

1913 - Photograph of Carl Thompson with one of Teetor's "Cars". Carl was doing soil survey work in northern Wisconsin for the University of Wisconsin Soils Dept.

Photograph shared by Carl's nephew Arthur E. Peterson who says about his uncle, "he was killed 4 weeks before the end of World War I in France. I never knew him, but my mother's stories of his work inspired me to study soils." Arthur may be reached at the University of Wisconsin-Madison, Soil Science Dept.

THE WAR CYCLE — Designed and built in Cape Town, South Africa, and used for scouting, dispatch riding, and ambulance work. It consists of two quadruplets, rigidly coupled with light iron, and fitted with flanged wheels and pneumatic tires. The "War Cycle" carried several men on the coupling framework in addition to the eight pedalers and was capable of speeds in excess of 30 miles per hour.

The preceding pages contain only a sampling of dozens of railbike and related patents that have been granted. And for every patented design, there are undoubtedly dozens of successful designs that have gone unpatented.

During the flurry of railbike development activity in the late 1800's, inventors seem to have been aware of each other's designs and made adaptations to create their own interpretation of existing railbikes. This is in contrast to more recent inventors, each whom felt that they had "discovered" the concept of the railbike and started more or less from scratch.

While this, no doubt, involved some re-invention of design elements which had already been tested and refined, this fresh approach has resulted in modern designs which have rapidly advanced railbike technology.

The next chapter provides an overview of the current status of railbiking, 100 years after its birth.

RAILBIKE

RAILBIKING TODAY

Let me join countless railbike enthusiasts who have preceded me during the past 100 years in saying, "Railbiking's time has come. There's growing interest and more miles of track are becoming available everyday. Railbike designs are better than ever and more and more people are riding the rails."

These statements are as true today as they've ever been. Yet why don't we see railbikes on everyone's Christmas list?

It certainly isn't because of a lack of railbike technology. Thanks to the support of organizations like the International Human Powered Vehicle Association (IHPVA) and the continuing efforts of enthusiasts across the country, railbikes have evolved into safe, durable rail vehicles.

So why don't you see railbikes at your local bike shop?

MODERN RAILBIKE - Romeo Gridelli's entry in the HPV Championships near Laupen, Switzerland, August 26, 1994.

Photo by Richard Smart

Liability.

More than any one reason, the possibility of injury or trespass has hampered what you might expect to be rapid growth fueled by popular demand. And in a litigation-happy society, this is no surprise.

Railroad companies understandably feel they have enough problems and little to gain by supporting the use of abandoned rails. Prospective railbike manufacturers see rapid sales overshadowed by personal injury lawsuits. So a stalemate exists.

The irony of the situation is that there is finally an abundance of abandoned rails available for railbikers to enjoy. But without popular support and a successful commercial railbike operation to promote growth, railbiking remains a well-kept secret. As the railbikers in the next chapter explain better than I can, this is a most unfortunate waste of a very special recreational resource.

Katrin Ranger (Germany), Low Tech Train, HPV Championships near Laupen, Switzerland, August 26, 1994.

Photo by Richard Smart

And the longer abandoned rails sit unused, the more they tend to "disappear." Every year miles of track are ripped up or buried to make way for urban expansion and suburban sprawl.

I experienced this on a personal level in testing and photographing my railbike models for this book. I returned to the site of my original railbike adventure to find the tunnel barricaded, but the tracks still usable.

But in the space of a few months, the tracks which we had enjoyed for decades were unceremoniously buried with dirt during the widening of an adjoining freeway. Bummer.

Multiply this by the number of freeway widenings, housing projects, and industrial park developments occurring every day and you get a feel for why it's a good idea to protect and save our abandoned rail resources before they are gone.

In this country there is a safe, convenient way to find plenty of abandoned railroad rights-of-way to use —

Tunnel #3 and tracks near San Quentin was the site of my first railbike rides.

over 83,000 miles of them. "Right-Of-Way - A Guide to Abandoned Railroads in the United States" (Maverick Publications, Bend, OR) is a publication which identifies abandoned tracks and their location. Now in its third edition, "Right-Of-Way" provides a listing, by state, which includes the name of the railroad, the end points of the abandoned section, the mileage between the end points, and the approximate date of abandonment. A map indicates the location of each of the abandoned rail lines.

"Right-Of-Way" was written by Waldo J. Nielsen, a native of New York, whose his interests included hiking, bicycling and local history. He was the First President of the Rochester (NY) Bicycling Club.

In 1966, Nielsen and friend Ralph Colt were planning a 50 mile hike, an activity much publicized due to President Kennedy's interest if physical fitness. It occurred to these men that abandoned railroad rights-of-way were ideal paths for such a hike.

Tunnel #3 is now boarded up. The rails were unceremoniously buried during the widening of nearby freeway.

After his hike, Nielsen began compiling a listing of all abandoned railroads in New York State. This listing was so well-received that Nielsen proceeded to prepare similar listings for all of the United States.

"Right-Of-Way" is a valuable reference, not just for railbikers, but for any individual or organization having an interest in the thousands of miles of abandoned railroads which crisscross America. The book explains the abandonment history and process in the United States and describes how the state listings were compiled. It includes several anecdotal examples of use of abandoned rail lines and provides a sense of the enjoyment that awaits adventurous railbikers.

You should understand that railroad "abandonment" is a legal process wherein the railroad company applies to the Interstate Commerce Commission for permission to abandon a specific segment of track. The ICC approves most applications and notifies state clearinghouses when an abandonment is filed. The complete process has many steps and implications. I mention this just so you have a feel for some of what is behind that set of tracks you may be considering for your railbike adventure. They may look abandoned, but in fact may still be "active." It's best to check first.

No discussion of abandoned railroad use would be complete without mentioning Rails-to-Trails Conservancy. The mission of this national non-profit organization is to enhance America's communities and countrysides by converting thousands of miles of abandoned railroad corridors, and connecting open space, into a national network of public trails.

As of mid-1995, more than 675 trails totalling nearly 7,000 miles have already been saved through the Conservancy as trails for recreation, transportation and open space conservation. But for every rail-trail that is saved, dozens of other abandoned railroad rights-of-way are lost to parking lots, highways or haphazard development.

Rails-to-Trails Conservancy is every cyclist's friend. More than 150,000 miles of rail corridor have been abandoned, and abandonments continue at a rate of 2,000 miles per year. Preservation of these corridors as connecting trails is important. You may wish to contact the Conservancy (See Appendix) to explore supporting or getting involved in rail-trail conservation in your community.

While railbikers support the concept and efforts of the Conservancy, they prefer, of course, that rails are left in tact on the rights-of-ways that are saved from development. This not only allows railbike use in concert with joggers, hikers and conventional cyclists, but also avoids the release of class-B carcinogens released into the soil and ground water during the disruption and removal of creosote-saturated railroad ties.

Though railbiking has yet to gain a foothold in the United States, other countries have enjoyed commercial railbike activities for years. An example is the vacation resort in Bengtsfors, Sweden which provides railbike rentals to visiting tourists to enjoy the surrounding countryside on the abandoned rails which border the resort.

This picture's so bad nobody gets credit.

This resort in Bengtsfors, Sweden features railbike rides on abandoned rails.

Railbike activist Michael Rohde (see next chapter) is attempting to establish a similar operation in cooperation with the Port of Tillamook, Washington. When successful, Mr. Rohde will provide us with the first railbike rental facility in the United States, complete with the breathtaking scenery of the Pacific Northwest.

In its August 12, 1995 news special on the plight of short-run railroads, NBC News focussed on the Tillamook line as an example of a railroad unable to maintain itself due to changes in demand for the raw materials it was built to transport. More than 300 similar "mom and pop" railroads have long been subsidized by the federal "Local Railfrieght Assistance Program". The trucking industry naturally feels such subsidies are unfair, and Congress wants to stop funding these lines.

Commercial railbike use of these lines offers a viable alternative to the wasting of this national resource. The railbikers whose interviews are in the following chapter would welcome access to these short run lines when they become available.

This type of railbike is used at the resort in Bengtsfors, Sweden.

RAILBIKERS

Instead of writing a book where I explain what I think railbiking is all about, I wanted to assemble something that offers many different viewpoints in describing this special activity.

The railbikers whose interviews appear on the following pages represent a sampling of active rail riders who share a fascination for the sport. They include regular family-man type guys as well as what I consider "adventurers." But each seems drawn to railbiking by a common attraction which combines the peace and solitude of the rails with the challenge and energy of cycling.

Each rider created the content of his interview himself and shared what he felt was important. By reading the stories these cyclists have to tell, I hope you will see that although they are all talking about the same activity, railbiking has come to mean something different to each of them.

The stories begin with the experiences of the only one in the group who is deceased. William Gillum has gone on to ride where all rails are abandoned and railbikes have replaced cars. He's first on the list only because he introduced me to railbiking when I saw him in Popular Mechanics 20 years ago and I said, "Hey, I can do that."

This is my favorite part of the book. It's the part that makes the subject come alive because it is written by real people, today, about real things they do. I hope their stories give you a feel for what railbiking is.

———————○———————

RAILBIKE

WILLIAM J. GILLUM
Colorado Springs, CO

In 1975 William Gillum went prospecting in the Colorado mountains. He had carried his equipment up a steep mountainside and was resting near an abandoned railroad when a fellow prospector, an Englishman he later learned, came around the bend pushing a little home-made cart on the rails. It had three bicycle wheels, two on one rail and one on the other and the tires had little flanges on their insides, just like train wheels. The whole thing folded in the middle and could be packed in the trunk of a car. The cart carried all of the Englishman's equipment – he wasn't even winded. Upon seeing this, Gillum felt many things, primarily envy.

Being a self-styled inventor, William wondered, 'Why don't I make one of these?' and 'Instead of pushing the cart, why not pedal it?' – The idea for Gillum's railbike was born.

"I had never seen a railbike and I thought I had come up with something new and unique," recalled Gillum. "But I've been through that before, with other inventions." So William began a patent search to see if his idea was really new.

The patent search showed that he was not first to invent the railbike – not even close. Scores of railbike patents had been issued during the late 1800's and early 1900's. "These old patents used every design I had cherished as original." said Gillum.

He nonetheless started work on his own version of a railbike. His first efforts were to fit metal rims to the sides of bicycle tires. The rims straddled the rail and the flanges made them roll straight and true. The front wheel of the old English 3-speed bicycle was locked with a bolt through them stem so it would steer straight and not turn left or right.

The first trial was a disaster. Gillum explained that he failed to observe a basic principle of bicycle engineering – you keep a bicycle upright by steering the front wheel toward the direction you are falling!

But his next design proved to be a winner. This three-wheeled outrigger design used 8-inch wheels with rubber tires which had wide grooves cut into the tires. Two of the wheels were fixed next to the front and rear bicycle wheels so they fit on the edges of the rail. The third wheel was mounted at the end of the outrigger at an angle so it rode on the inside edge of the other rail. Gillum used 3/4 inch steel tubing

with copper plumbing fittings and nuts and bolts – all things available at any hardware store.

He used his new railbike extensively over the next few months, seeking media coverage to help spread the

Photograph by Mary Rocha

This Popular Mechanics picture of Mr. Gillum in 1976 made him an overnight railbike celebrity.

This is the original railbike built by William J. Gillum in 1975.

word. His first story appeared in the December, 1975 issue of *Harper's Weekly* as a feature story. In February 1976 *Popular Mechanics* included Gillum and his railbike in its "It's New Now" section as a news item.

Over the next few months William received over 2,000 inquiries from all over the world. Calls and letters came from cyclists, railroad enthusiasts, engineers, scientists, colleges and universities and even one from General

Motors' design shop. Dozens of other inventors who had already built their own railbikes also contacted Mr. Gillum.

William founded the American Railbike Association (ARA) and members received a booklet containing an overview of all of the research Gillum had done on railbikes. The news clippings, photographs, patent drawings and advice provided in the booklet got prospective railbikers off to a good start.

Photograph by Mary Rocha

Gillum mounted a guide wheel at an angle next to each bicycle wheel.

Mr. Gillum observed that two basic questions always seemed to come up. First, how could people get construction plans to build their own railbike? And second, where could they get information about abandoned railroads.

To answer the first question, Mr. Gillum included in the ARA member booklet plans for building a "new and improved" railbike. It uses two bicycles, one on each rail. He stated that this design "provided stability that simply is not possible with a single

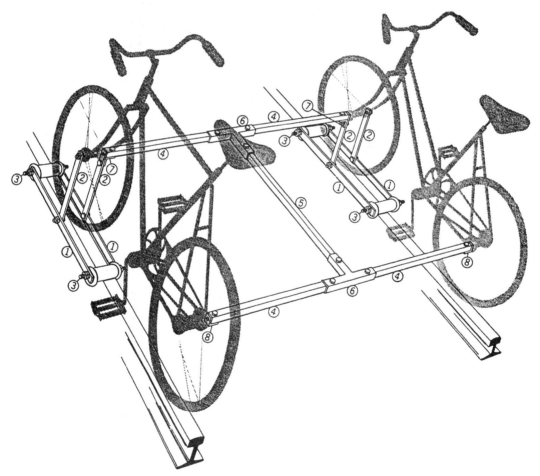

The two-bike design Gillum included in his ARA handbook provided a sort of cradle for the front wheels of each bicycle.

bike, outrigger design." And most importantly, he explained, "the two bike design provided a means to deal with the unfortunate fact that the distance between rails does vary."

He answered the second question by becoming a distributor for a book by Waldo Nielsen entitled "Right-Of-Way - A Guide to Abandoned Railroads in the United States." ARA members

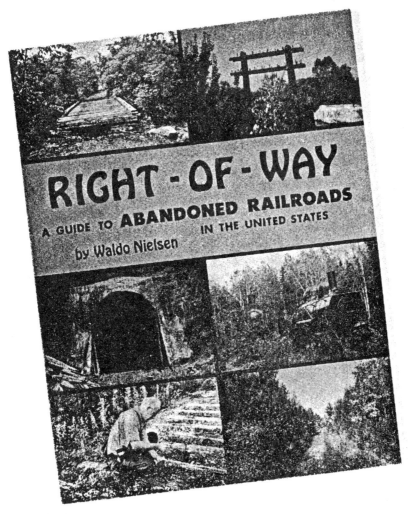

This 1st edition of "Right-Of-Way" listed 35,000 miles of abandoned tracks. The current edition contains 83,000 miles.

could purchase a copy of this guide with their membership. This book is currently in its third revised edition and is a valuable resource to railbikers. (See Appendix - Resources chapter) The book provides the location of

nearly 84,000 miles of abandoned railroads throughout the United States.

Mr. Gillum believed that "almost anyone can adapt an ordinary bicycle to run on abandoned railroad tracks." He

Gillum's American Railbike Association member handbook showed tandem railbikers enjoying the rails.

said that with some conviction because he had seen it done "in a backyard, using common materials and ordinary tools and equipment." It requires some attention to detail, he explained, but "it is not all that difficult."

"The one big consideration is to provide a guiding system that assures the railbike will stay on the rails," Gillum stated, "even when the rails become more than the standard 56¼ inches apart." He felt this was essential if the railbike was to have a touring capability and that his two-bike design was the only design to accomplish this.

William Gillum died in 1980. His wife Lyllian describes him as a tireless tinkerer and inventor who enjoyed making things and loved sharing them with people. She adds that his one weakness was a somewhat naive approach to business. Gillum and partner Harry Kevis invented a product called "POWR" — a solution which brought dead car batteries back to life.

They traveled extensively to auto shows and exhibitions promoting this miracle battery elixer that really worked. They almost made it onto The Tonight Show with their invention, but the product never got off the ground and was added to William's list of 'great ideas that would someday make a million.'

I guess we all have our own great idea list, but Gillum's seems longer than most. He eventually ran out of money to promote his "POWR" product and put it to rest.

But his railbike work has been an inspiration for many to follow and has guided the development of continued refinements over the years. When she learned that William would be included in this book, Lyllian Gillum wrote to me to say, "I am proud that my husband's work will be once again in evidence."

So am I.

FLORIAN GRENIER
Quebec, Canada

The grandfather of modern railbiking is still an active rider who has logged over 6,000 kilometers on bikes he has designed and built himself. Florian Grenier built his first railbike in 1945 and continues to refine and test-ride his designs.

Florian explains that he built his second railbike in 1952 but, "at that moment, the railroad was expanding and I had to stop my travels because of traffic. But in 1982 I built my third one and started to make excursions on many of the abandoned tracks before they dismantled them."

"I built my fourth railbike in 1986 (this is the one I am presently using) and I built another design in 1994," says Florian. (Based on 50 years of personal railbiking experience.)

Florian describes the evolution of his design: "At first I was using flanges with the wheels but that made too much noise. Later I substituted small,

Florian Grenier en route from Canterberry to McAdam, New Brunswick, Canada.

six-inch wheels on each side of the track but the wheels took too much space and were unable to cross roadways, switches, etc."

Mr. Grenier continues, "I modified that design and used skateboard wheels. At first I fixed them at about 45° to the track and later on I mounted them vertically. The first year I used this design the wheels were non-retractable, but after another year I was able to make them retractable which was very useful for crossing roads and switches."

"One thing I learned from the beginning," Florian states, "if you want a solid design, your outrigger has to hold on to the bike at three points, like a triangle. If not, you lose solidity."

He points out that he is able to carry baggage on his outrigger, but not more than ten pounds. He packs most of his gear on the bike itself.

Here's a guy with some railbiking miles under his belt. About 4,000 of them. His longest trip was in British Columbia on the BC Rail North

Photograph by Florian Grenier

To reach "end of steel" at Chipmunk, Florian and party flew to Mosque to begin their 237 mile railbike adventure.

between Chipmunk (end of steel) and Fort St. James — a distance of 237 miles. Another totalled 186 miles between Cochrane and Moosone Ontario and a third between Souix Lookout and Conmee in northwestern Ontario added another 186 miles to his total. On some trips Florian brings his "partners" Michel Raiche and Marcel Charette-Yvon Côté on bikes he built.

Florian Grenier's attraction to railbiking is simple, "My railbike gives me plenty of satisfaction and I may go wherever I want."

He has written a book about his railbike designs, and experiences and you may order it directly from him for $22. Canadian including shipping:

Florian Grenier
CP 128 Sullivan
Quebec, Canada J0Y 2N0.

His book is written entirely in French but contains wonderful photographs of his adventures. It's worth the price for the pictures alone, and is a real bargain if you can find someone who can read it to you.

Photograph by Florian Grenier

Armed with a machete, Florian clears the path to reach the "end of steel."

RICHARD SMART
Coeur d'Alene, ID

If there's one person who can be considered the driving force behind modern-day railbiking, Richard Smart is the one. He has been called the "father and chief proponent" of the sport, and he has the credentials to prove it.

No other railrider begins to approach Richard's 25,000 miles logged on the tracks, and no one else I came across could produce such an overwhelming library of railbiking information including research, news clippings, videos, interviews and networking contacts.

Most importantly, Dr. Smart (he's a dentist by trade) is willing to share what he has in the interest of promoting the sport he loves.

"Railbiking is a wonderful sport and I don't want it abused," says Richard. And he goes out of his way to

Photography by Richard Smart

Inventor of the "Railcycle", Richard C. Smart at Eagle's Nest tunnel via Montana Canyon in 1982.

do what's right for the orderly, responsible evolution of his sport.

Smart began railbiking in 1975 and has continued his love affair with the rails ever since. Unlike other railbikers who seem to dabble at the design challenges involved, Richard hasn't taken any short cuts.

He began by developing and refining a working railbike and obtaining a patent for it in 1980. This in itself requires a monumental effort and a major financial investment.

Many of us would stop there, but Richard continued refining his patented design to evolve a lighter weight, more portable design. He founded "Smart Railcycles" to market his railbike and orders started arriving at his door. He sold 29 Railcycles before a string of intimidating letters from railroad officials convinced him to suspend production.

"I felt just like the upstart automobile maker 'Tucker' in the movie," said Smart of the experience. So all of that investment has been put on hold.

Credit Smithsonian Institution

This picture from George B. Adbill's "This Was Railroading" was Dr. Smart's original inspiration.

Photography by Richard Smart

1986 Christmas Card: The Richard Smart Family (l.to r.) Richard, wife Ann, Mike, Tom, Jim, Jenny. Dogs - Butch, Toby

Plans to build your own Railcycle are available, however (See Appendix). And, as you might expect, the plans are excellent. Twelve oversized pages of detailed blueprints leave nothing to the imagination in guiding you to construct a first class Railcycle attachment for your bicycle.

Smart's patented Railcycle design is a marvel. A single large guide wheel is mounted along side the rail and two skateboard-size travel wheels ride on top of the rail. Two metal flanges extend down along each side of the rail for added security.

Two magnets are slung between the travel wheels, 1/8 inch above the rail. With 60 pounds of magnetic pull and a slight outward angling of the travel wheels, the guide wheel rides perfectly on the inside of the track. There's so little friction that the bike will coast 20 feet with a slight push.

A telescoping outrigger with a leveling control keeps the bike upright and the whole system folds up to allow riding the bike to and from the tracks.

Did I mention Smart is thorough? His plans include a sales agreement you must sign before you take delivery of the plans. This agreement includes your legal promise to use your Railcycle "only on abandoned track with proper permission." Once again, Richard is trying to guide the growth of the sport he loves.

Your Railcycle plans also come with a list of "Riding Tips and Courte-

sies" to help you respect the private property of the railroads and others you might encounter on your railbike adventures. These are the kinds of things you'll find woven through your dealings with Richard Smart – an unceasing commitment to protecting his sport from being overrun by a bunch of "Yahoo's."

Dozens of media events and newspaper and magazine articles have chronicled Smart's adventures and Railcycle development work. When I first contacted Richard and told him about

Credit Smithsonian Institution

This picture, taken in the early 1900's, is one of Richard Smart's favorites.

Photography by Richard Smart

70 miles north of Ely, Nevada, Richard Smart pauses on a 150 mile trip through the desert.

my writing this book, I asked him if he had any information he could share with me. He said, "Sure, I'll send you some stuff."

The next week a large box arrived containing dozens of photographs, hundreds of pages of stories, a video and some booklets. All neatly categorized and arranged in their own folders. I later learned that this was only a small part of his railbike library.

Smart's seemingly endless stream of interests surrounding his railbike

passion includes his rail and nail collections. On his various railbiking adventures, Richard collects discarded chunks of rail and the increasingly rare railroad tie date nails that he might encounter.

"Every length of rail bears the identification of the foundry that produced it along with its weight and date of manufacture," explains Smart. For instance, in his neck of the woods he has found "Illinois Steel Works VI 1893 72.2." This means that particular length of rail was made by the Illinois

Steel Works foundry in June of 1893 and a three foot length weighs 72.2 pounds. "Weights are always given per three foot length. I think the heaviest is about 140 pounds per three feet," Richard adds, "The lightest I have seen is only 60 pounds — the weight of the rails used for the first transcontinental railroad."

He explained that some of the oldest rail he has found came from England as ballast in the bottoms of the old sailing ships. Some of these older rails still serve as safety rails on old bridges and trestles. The oldest rail that Smart has seen was an 1872 rail that he spotted while railcycling with Florian Grenier in Quebec. Much of this very old rail was replaced by newer, heavier rails.

Smart also boasts an impressive collection of date nails whose heads are debossed with the year in which they were driven into place. His oldest date nail is 1908. The railroads did this to keep track of how long ties would last. Each railroad had its own style of date nail, some made of copper, some of steel. Richard mentioned that there are books devoted to the complicated study and collection of date nails.

As Dr. Smart began to explain the various types of pole nails (marked and dated nails driven into the old telegraph poles) he's gathered, I knew it was time to get back to our discussion of railbiking and save a more complete review of his hobbies and packrat tendencies for another time. (Can you imagine what his garage must look like?)

Richard Smart has several unique railbiking credentials to add to the D.D.S. that follows his name:

First, he invented the term "RAILCYCLE", which, I predict, will earn a spot in everyone's dictionary,

Second, Smart should be credited for developing the first practical railbike that can be easily ridden on rails and roads.

Third, and perhaps most importantly, he has invested himself in the responsible nurturing of the sport he helped so much to create. In a world where information is power and liability is everywhere, he has shared his knowledge and experience so we all might enjoy railbiking in a safe and legal environment.

"I do it for the adventure, the solitude, to see the scenery and wildlife, and for the exercise," Smart explains. "I've been through hundreds of tunnels, some so dark you couldn't see your hand. I carry history books with me and when we get to little towns, we read up on their history and go to their museums. We learn about the people."

Smart grew up in a small town in Montana where the mail and packages came by rail. "Railroads brought us these wonderful things," Smart says. "When we walk down the tracks, we dream about all the places the railroad can take you."

The rails still give Richard Smart a sense of wonder and each railbike trip is an adventure. He never outgrew his love for the railroads, and future generations of railbikers can be glad that he didn't.

Here's Dr. Smart's Railcycle logo.

MICHAEL ROHDE
Olympia, WA

Michael was introduced to railbiking by the book "Pedal Power" (Rodale Press) in the early 1980's. For him there was an elegance and simplicity about it. For years the image of pedaling silently on rails through the countryside stuck in his mind. Michael explains his continuing interest in railbiking:

"In 1991 I was in Costa Rica working on a project to help raise funds for the purchase of a pristine rain forest near the southern port town of Golfito. While in Golfito I noticed some rusty narrow gauge tracks that had been used to move bananas from the plantations to the loading dock at the port. These tracks ran out of town for about 70 miles, at times within a few hundred yards of four national parks and wildlife refuges."

"By the time I began to seriously consider the idea of developing railbiking tours in Costa Rica it was 1994. I called my friend Carlos Evans, who was

Michael Rohde and best friend railbike past the beautiful miniature "sea stacks" north of Tillamook Bay, Oregon.

Photography by Ann Story

the director of an economic development agency in the Golfito area. The news was immediately devastating: the tracks had been pulled up for scrap only 8 months earlier. As an afterthought I asked Carlos if there was any other track that might be suitable. He told me that the "Jungle Train" which ran from San Jose in the Central Valley to the Atlantic port town of Limon was abandoned after a 1991 earthquake."

"After gathering as much information as possible from a distance, I traveled to Costa Rica to meet with some government officials and get a firsthand look at the tracks. The track was in terrible condition. I finally focused on a section of track that was only 13 kilometers long and came complete with a landslide and rail that disappeared for kilometers under 10 foot high grasses and shrubs. It was apparent that any venture would require large sums of money for track repair. This, combined with a lack of response from initially enthusiastic government officials after I returned to the U.S., caused me to finally give up on the Costa Rica venue."

"In spite of this inauspicious beginning and the sometimes well-meaning skepticism of co-workers, family and friends, I embarked on a search for suitable track somewhere in the world. The philosophy of being infinitely flexible and approaching apparent problems by looking for ways to make them assets (while still being able to face reality and walk away if necessary) has lead me to consider many interesting parts of the world in my search for track. These include the island of St. Kitts in the Caribbean, 36 miles of light gauge track around the perimeter of the island; Sakhalin Island in eastern Russia, hundreds of miles of tracks abandoned decades ago, condition unknown; an abandoned line in the Andes in Ecuador, reopened for a brief time in 1994 and subsequently closed due to lack of profits; Spain - rumors of track in the Pyrenees overlooking the Mediterranean; Portugal and most recently, Tillamook, Oregon - which is in my own back yard."

"My experience with the short haul Tillamook Line (Tillamook to Banks), owned and operated by the Port of Tillamook Bay, has been very positive. Communities on the Oregon Coast have experienced a serious downturn in their local economies in recent years due to restrictions in fishing and log-

The 100-mile Tillamook line. (Map courtesy of The Northwest Rail Museum, Box 19342, Portland, Oregon, 97280)

ging, cnvironmental concerns and the cyclic nature of these markets. The Port of Tillamook has been laying off employees due to these pressures but the Port has shown vision in its efforts to find new ways to remain profitable. I view possible agreements to develop railbiking in this area as an important opportunity for railbiking and the local economy which is relying more and more on tourism."

"The Port of Tillamook has allowed me to railbike on their track to assess it for potential railbike tours. My wife and I were able to sign a waiver of liability (see copy in SAFETY chapter) which is one of the main sticking points when using railroad property. According to one Port employee, this waiver has been used and upheld in Federal Court for activities such as bungee jumping and paragliding. The Port's attorneys reviewed it and determined that it would, in their opinion, hold up under Oregon State law. This type of waiver, if found effective, could be very useful for rail-

Photography by Ann Story

Michael Rohde (left) and friend at the Port of Tillamook, Oregon.

Northern Portugal — Railbikes in front of the Arco de Baúlhe Station on the Tamega rail line.

Photography by Carlos Martins de Fonseca

bikers and others who approach liability-wary corporations and individuals. It is important that anyone using this waiver have it examined by local attorneys to determine its potential effectiveness in case of tort claims resulting in death or injury while using corporate property."

"It is important to get permission from owners/operators of track not only out of courtesy, but also as an important safety measure (not to mention criminal trespass laws). When my wife and I signed the waiver, we spoke to the dispatcher who was able to tell us that no trains were running that day and alerted track maintenance workers that we would be out on the track. I also wore a high-visibility orange safety vest as a precaution for motor vehicles at road crossings."

"The experience of railbiking on the Oregon Coast near Tillamook was one of the highlights of my life. The natural beauty and wildlife were incredible. We saw places along the coast that people in cars don't ever get a chance to see. The most amazing part of the trip, however, was the response of the people we met along the way. We had planned to make a 28 mile round trip, but ended up doing slightly less than 20. In areas where we could be seen from Highway 101, and at road crossings in towns, people wanted to talk to us about the bikes and what we were doing. Some people actually turned around on the highway and caught up with us to talk. In an area where you might think that the locals could be a little jaded by the tourist industry, the people we met couldn't have been more supportive. We also spoke with a number of bicyclists who were making the trip down Highway 101. Seeing them in traffic made me very glad to be on the tracks."

"I have visited Portugal and met with two university professors who have been organizing walking tours of abandoned narrow gauge lines. When I first contacted them, they immediately saw the possibilities of railbiking as a better way to move tourists. We railbiked several different narrow gauge lines (with the permission of Portuguese Railways) to evaluate them for possible railbike tours. The scenery and history of these abandoned lines offer another opportunity for development of railbiking and I am optimistic about the prospects."

"I want to acknowledge the support, encouragement and friendship of Richard Smart whose design I am using to develop the railbike model I plan to use for tours. His magnetic design and telescopic outrigger are nothing short of genius."

"In order to come up with a configuration that would lend itself to being used by people with no railbiking experience, I have added a few features to Richard's original design and omitted others. I don't consider these additions to be "improvements" - Richard's 25,000 plus miles of railbiking speak for the viability of his design."

"At the beginning, Richard Smart and I had talked about what I call a side-by-side tandem, consisting of two mountain bikes, one over each rail, joined by an outrigger system. Richard had experimented successfully with this configuration in the 1970's and had once hooked several tandems together in a "train" that had worked quite well."

"The first outrigger system I designed had a sliding joint between the bikes which made them very fast to set up. I also imagined that it would take up any difference in the distance between the rails as it traveled. Unfortunately my 'innovation' was too clever for its own good, causing occasional derailments of the rear tires. I have since gone to a rigid outrigger."

"My main contribution to Richard Smart's magnetic system is a redesign of the magnet itself. Richard had used alnico magnets made in Great Britain which were expensive, especially if you bought them one or two at a time. To reduce the cost of the magnets, I talked to a number of magnet manufacturers about different possibilities. Some were polite but confused, and others (on commission I suppose) insisted that the only way to go was to use very expensive rare earth magnets. I finally discovered an advertisement in the Edmund Scientific catalog which offered a small ceramic magnet with "pole pieces" that move the pole closer

Photography by Ann Story

Rohde's "Outrigger #1" with sliding connector joint for the side-by-side tandem.

together in some configurations which concentrates the magnetic field. The ad stated that the ceramic magnet alone would pick up about three pounds, while adding the pole pieces enabled it to pick up many times that weight."

"This clue, not mentioned in any of the magnetics books or articles I have read, lead me to design a large, relatively inexpensive, ceramic magnet with pole pieces and a very strong pull. In the end there were other advantages over the alnico horseshoe magnets. My design fits up inside the magnetic carriage housing, uses two mounting bolts instead of one which prevents the magnet from turning while being mounted, and has poles that are several inches long. This translates into more holding area. They are also not prone to demagnetizing."

"Other design changes I've made include a 'bounce limiter' to keep the magnetic carriage from bouncing too high when it hits a bad rail end. It is spring loaded to make it return to the rail faster. A "steering limiter" (suggested to me by Smart) uses aircraft cable. This reduces the problem of inexperienced riders oversteering if the guide wheel wanders momentarily. Finally, I have developed a universal fork mounting system that attaches the magnetic carriage to the front axle of the bicycle instead of to the front forks. This makes it possible to use almost any bike with little or no redesign necessary."

"Developing commercial guided tours may not seem like a glamorous way to help popularize the sport, but I believe this approach will provide visibility and legitimacy for railbiking. It seems like the only way to get the attention and support of the people and institutions that railbikers ultimately rely on - those who own the tracks and rights of way. I am hopeful that as railbiking is accepted as a commercial option for preserving rail corridors, opportunities will also open up for independent railbikers, who will be viewed as a resource to attract tourist dollars, rather than pesky trespassers and liability risks. Of course, this means that courtesy and responsibility on the part of commercial tour operators and independent railbikers will need to be scrupulously observed."

"No matter where abandoned railroad tracks might be, I believe that the

key to preserving rail corridors and developing railbiking as something other than a curiosity is to find ways to develop it commercially. This means providing an economic incentive to leave the tracks in place and to this end railbiking can have a significant role to play."

———— ○ ————

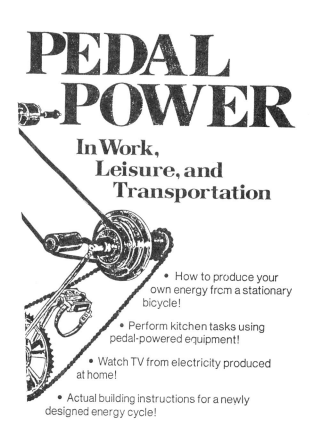

PEDAL POWER

In Work, Leisure, and Transportation

- How to produce your own energy from a stationary bicycle!
- Perform kitchen tasks using pedal-powered equipment!
- Watch TV from electricity produced at home!
- Actual building instructions for a newly designed energy cycle!

Michael Rohde's obsession with railbiking started innocently enough — he read "Pedal Power".

(Published by Rodale Press and edited by James C. McCullagh, 1977.)

RON FORSTER
Antrim, PA

While most railbikers pursue their sport for the sheer joy of it, Ron Forster has focussed his interest on a higher level. He started out as others before him, but ended up involved in a more noble effort — Ron adapted railbiking for use by the blind and handicapped. Here's how he tells it:

"I guess I'm like the thousands of railriders before me - I saw a need and filled it. The abandoned tracks were there and I needed to ride them. It wasn't until months after I took my first ride that I found out that someone else had already done it over a hundred years before me."

"My friend Rudy and I thought up plans for our first rider over lunch one day. We worked all afternoon and into the night welding, bending, and creating. I think it was somewhere around midnight, with flashlights taped to the frame, that we tested our masterpiece

Ron Forster pedals through a New Hampshire snowfall on a "conventional" outrigger-type railbike.

on the tracks. It worked well but required two men and a donkey to lift it on and off the tracks. By the light of the silvery moon I could see what was and was not needed for the railrider I ultimately wanted."

"I felt it was easy to figure out – I just looked at train wheels. They all had flanges, so that's the direction I went, too."

"The next few days found me at a friend's Bridgeport milling machine. I bought a five foot long, five inch round piece of plastic, cut it up, and proceeded to make the angles that would allow a double flange wheel to be the guiding system for the perfect railbike. In a few days I had it. The Double Flange 200 (DF 200) was created. I've been using it ever since."

"A reporter for the Manchester Union Leader saw me on the tracks and did a story. At that point things just got crazy – everybody wanted to do a story about this bike I 'invented'."

"I was contacted by syndicated radio and newspaper news services. In 1983 they started doing stories that appeared all over the world. I did a half-hour TV talk show on one of our

Here's what Ron Forster's cast aluminum railrider wheels look like up close.

local stations. *World Weekly News, Mother Earth, People, Yankee, Bicycling, Wall Street Journal* – I spent a day with the NBC Nightly News crew, even the Japanese sent a TV crew over!"

"All this media attention started an avalanche of inquiries on "how to build one." People from all over the world also sent me pictures of the bikes they or their fathers built. Sadly I learned I really wasn't the first person to invent the railbike."

"Being an entrepreneur, I saw an opportunity. People wanted information on how to build their own railbikes and needed the wheels to guide them. With all the information people sent me, and from what I found through research, I wrote my book which I called 'RAIL RIDERS'." (See APPENDIX for ordering information)

"Over the years I've sold the book, and wheels to people all over the world. I feel this is the most rewarding thing about railriding, meeting people who have the same interest as I have."

"I have attached my SF 100 and DF 200 wheels to many kinds of bikes including the two wheeler I like the most, the recumbent (reclining) design. Since it has a lower center of gravity, it rides the curves much better. When I first looked at the recumbent, I guessed that the back wheel wouldn't track very well on a railroad track. But I quickly learned that even with the greater distance between the front and back wheels, it performed well. And since it is recumbent, it is easier to pedal."

"One beautiful sunny day I was gliding along on my railbike without a care in the world. For some reason, I stopped, sat up on the handle bars facing backwards, and tried pedaling."

"It worked! I immediately thought 'GUINESS!' I could be the first person to ride a bicycle, on railroad tracks, backwards. Surely the GUINESS Book of World Records wouldn't have anyone who had done this."

"But their letter came back, 'Sorry, not interested.' They turned me down, but that day I learned that you didn't have to <u>see</u> to ride a railbike."

"It was a great day! At that moment I realized that railriding could open up a new sport to millions of people who couldn't see. This segment

of our population had limited recreational activities available to them."

"I tested this theory on myself and rode with my eyes closed. I asked my blind friend Ray if he would agree to be a guinea pig. He couldn't wait to give it a try."

"Even with the DF 200 wheels guiding the bike, one must still exert some steering pressure when encountering curves. My blind friend Ray, of course, couldn't see the curves, but for some reason I assumed he would be able to "feel" them better than a sighted person. I was wrong and the bike came off the tracks. No real damage, and I knew what needed to be done to solve the problem. So, back to the workshop we went."

"After studying the various designs which railbikers before me had built, I realized that a vehicle for the blind had to be a four-wheeler. My design would be as simple as possible, keeping the center of gravity low, using an "I-beam"

"RON'S RIDER" — "Simply the best rail bike in the world." — Ron Forster.

Photography by Ron Forster

11 boy- and girlscouts from the Perkins School for the Blind enjoying themselves on Ron's Railriders.

frame and four wheels — two on each track, to provide stability."

"I started searching for a light-weight wheel and found that the kind I wanted just didn't exist. So I decided to manufacture my own."

"There are several foundries in Franklin, New Hampshire, where my shop is located. The very first one I approached felt my quest to create a railrider for the blind was a noble cause. After a long weekend we came

up with a good design that now had to be built into a mold."

"After some expense in mold making and other related items, I had my wheel. A seventeen inch aluminum wheel weighing 11 pounds."

"I was, of course, excited when the day finally came to test my new, four-wheeled rider. I knew what success would mean — It wasn't just a nice ride down the tracks for me. Success would mean I could use my railrider to touch

the lives of a lot of people in a very positive way."

"Things went well that day. I had built a railrider that would allow every blind person to enjoy a new sport. I christened it 'RON'S RIDER'."

"I contacted the Perkins School for the Blind in Massachusetts and told them about my bicycle I had made for blind people. A few weeks later we met on 13 miles of track in Wolfboro, New Hampshire."

"I was nervous. I arrived just at the time we had agreed upon to unload the dozen railriders I had built just for this special event. I had gone riding with blind people before, but Perkins was bringing eleven blind children to ride all at once."

"After meeting the children, I gathered them around one rider to explain what they were going to experience. I had the boys and girls feel the rider and I answered their questions. The questions were few — they just

Courtesy of Ron Forster

A simple ramp provides easy railbike access from a wheelchair for Dave Lorden, Wilmot, New Hampshire.

Courtesy of Ron Forster

Blind since World War II, Art Newton of Franklin, New Hampshire, enjoys an afternoon on a railbike.

wanted to get onto their own rider and start experiencing what everyone had been telling them about."

"I learned a lot that day as I watched this caravan of blind railriders pedal up and down the tracks. Everything went well. Not one mishap."

"It was amazing. I had thought everyone would be bumping into one another. It was like they were guided by laser – they all kept a perfect distance from the rider in front of them. Nice things were said by those boys and girls that day, and I received many wonderful letters from them in the weeks following that historic day."

What could be better? Doing what you enjoy, and making people happier in the process?

RAILBIKE

PETER ALEXANDER
Kowloon, Hong Kong

Pete first started railbiking as a school kid and built his first railbike in the mid-sixties. His first railbike setup was fitted to a Moulton which he rode in England on an abandoned portion of the Oxford-Princes Risborough line.

The young Mr. Alexander continued to build quite a few models in the years that followed but interest waned after a while since most of the aban-

Somewhere in rural England Peter Alexander gives a ride to a stranded pedestrian. Pete had a British machine shop build this railbike for him. The wheels and drive unit are Swedish. (Photo courtesy of Richard Smart)

doned tracks had been removed. But since then more tracks have become available in the United Kingdom.

Pete explains, "While working in Scandinavia in the 70's and 80's my fascination with railbiking was renewed since there were many tracks available, especially in Sweden. Over the years I have kept an active interest and built many types of railbikes including those that run only on rails and also special kits that enable an ordinary bike to run on tracks."

Pete continues, "I have sold railbikes, but only if someone asked me to make one. I have sold a few to various places around the world including one to Alaska. Many people are put off from the sport of railbiking by the lack of a suitable machine. Either they cannot, or they are unwilling to build one from scratch.

If people are unable to participate, the sport will never take off. However, I have now produced a simple version which anyone can fit to a normal bike."

Pete Alexander is pals with Richard Smart and the two have corresponded about railbiking for more than ten years. Pete explains that they share a goal of "getting the sport 'out of the closet' and legally accepted, with tracks made available."

To that end Pete has started a newsletter called the *Railbike Express* which is published every two months. Cost and ordering information appears below as listed in the Classified section of the *HPV News.*

Railbikers come and go, but Peter Alexander is one of the few that have been around a long time, and are committed to the sport for the long run.

———————— ○ ————————

Classifieds

RAILBIKE

TOM WALZ
Bethlehem, Pennsylvania

A self-employed musician, Tom Walz is also a writer and, while on the staff of *Bicycling Magazine*, was assigned to research and write a piece about railbiking.

"As lowest writer on the totem pole of *Bicycling Magazine*, I got assigned all the weird stuff," recalls Tom. His assignments were leading him down the path to journalistic obscurity: "Out-of-round chainrings, stem shifter and 'safety' lever how's and why's, and then railbikes."

Tom's article "Rail Riders and their New Freedom Machine" appeared in *Bicycling*'s July 1983 issue. The good news is that Tom received

Musician/Railbiker Tom Walz cruises along some of Pennsylvania's abandoned rail lines.

Photography by Diane Dalton

Photography by Tom Walz

A turnbuckle allows height adjustment of the front guide wheel on Waiz's railbike.

lot's of feedback from *Bicycling*'s readers. The bad news is that all the responses were negative.

"I received some nasty letters from some very narrow-minded individuals," says Tom. "I didn't get one 'Oh, wow, cool' letter. I was bummed."

But while Tom's railbike assignment did little to advance his journal-

ism career, it has had a profound impact on his life nonetheless.

"Is this railbike thing a hobby for me or an obsession?" wonders Tom in a recent interview.

In researching his initial article 12 years ago, got Tom started on his own, "improved" designs. With input from fellow railbikers Ron Forster and

Richard Smart, Walz set up a simple shop and began building his own bike.

Tom started with the square tubing legs off a discarded construction barrier and the telescoping tubing from a clothes rack. He used a modified C-clamp to provide an adjustable height feature to his outrigger.

Low tech, but effective.

"It worked like a champ," says Tom. "I was just tickled with how well it performed. I rode about a hundred miles on this rig before the cyclist in me wanted more efficiency and more speed."

So Tom went back to the drawing board. He designed a new guide that was fast but, unfortunately, prone to sporadic and spectacular derailments.

Tom's "Low Tech" C-clamp allows adjustment of the outrigger's height.

Photography by Tom Walz

Still at the drawing board, Tom promises, "My next design will be fast <u>and</u> safe and will tolerate weeds and track debris."

Yet in his enthusiasm for railbiking, Mr. Walz goes out of his way to

Photography by Tom Walz

The single front guide wheel is mounted at an angle.

talk about safety: "I must stress that I don't take rail use lightly. I grew up in a railroad-loving family and have always lived within earshot of a railroad. I have been walking the rails since I was nine. I have trained my ears and eyes to recognize rail traffic. I can guess within a few days when a train has passed last on rusty rails. My rule of thumb is, 'If you can see your reflection in the rail, GET LOST !' Use only abandoned rails."

Tom continues, "Finally, I am against anyone mass manufacturing railbikes or the attachments for this activity. If they are sold to the general public, 'stupid' people will buy them and get hurt or killed. In today's litigious society they will probably sue the railroad for their own stupidity."

"It took a lot of time and effort, physically and mentally, to create my railbikes and I invest as much energy in using them safely," adds Mr. Walz. "If you want to ride a railbike, build one!"

Excellent advice.

—————— o ——————

ROBERT STORMS
Rochester, New York

The International Human Powered Vehicle Association (IHPVA) is just what you might guess – an organization made up of people involved in the study and development of vehicles that are powered by humans. Rob Storms is an active IHPVA member and advocate.

I had seen an article he had written in the *HPV NEWS* which chronicled his design and testing of various railbike configurations. His experience is particularly notable because he is one of the first railbike "activists" to document successful adaptation of a contemporary recumbent bicycle design for rail use. Though Rob's design was featured in the article, he is quick to point out that fellow railbiker Ron Forster had used a recumbent years earlier.

I caught up with Rob just before he left for the Netherlands for the annual

Rob Storms on his recumbent railbike, pauses to inspect his outrigger.

Arms folded to display their "no hands" capabilities, Rob Storms and friend part company as the tracks split.

Human Powered Vehicle Championships. In real life Rob is a partner in the Sound Source, an exceptional music store in Rochester – his fantasy life, however, revolves around human powered vehicles.

Rob describes his first railbike as an experiment. It was based on a Hypercycle which is a recumbent (reclining bicycle) with a very short wheelbase. He knew that recumbents would be well-suited to rail use since "you don't have as far to fall."

He made his outrigger tripod from electrical conduit and used wheels from a pull-type golf cart. A guide arm attached to the front axle held a vertically mounted skateboard wheel against the inside edge of the track. A big rubber band stretched to the end of one handlebar kept the guide wheel in contact with the track.

Rob recalls that, "When I would hit an unusually bad joint in the rail, the guide wheel would bounce sideways and launch the front fork into a violent

Courtesy of Rob Storms

One of Rob's pals takes his railbike for a spin.

turn, steering the bike off the track with the guide wheel digging a hole between the ties. Blood-letting would often follow as entropy took over."

Storms was undaunted by his the bruises earned during his learning curve and soon returned to the rails with refinements which vastly improved his railbike's performance. He adapted an Infinity brand recumbent, using an old bicycle fork with two skateboard wheels mounted in an inverted "V" which straddle the top

corners of the rail and steer the bike down the center.

The guide fork is spring-loaded to minimize bounce at bad rail joints. His three-legged outrigger is made of aluminum tubing with a skateboard truck mounted at the end. Its two skateboard wheels effectively form a single wide roller.

The outrigger comes off and stores folded under the seat, and the front guide swings up to allow riding the bike "off-track" to and from the rails. He says the whole set-up adds about ten pounds to the bike and folds up in about three minutes.

Rob displays his freewheeling imagination in contemplating future railbike designs: "I would like to get rid of the extra wheels and outrigger altogether, perhaps sensing the position of the rail magnetically and using a steering servo. The bike could be held upright by a steerable airplane-type tail rudder or perhaps by shifting some weights from side to side down near the tracks. Using only one rail would allow two-way traffic without the unsavory jousting that might otherwise occur."

Storms continues his interest in human powered vehicles and extends a standing offer to swap information and ideas with readers who wish to share experiences and fantasies. Why not give him a call?

———○———

Rob Storms (left) and friend enjoy a ride.

PAUL MORNINGSTAR
Creston, California

"I'm pretty much a full time environmentalist," explains Paul Morningstar. "You might have seen me in a 1990 PBS documentary "Forest through the Trees."

Paul is trying to remain a counter-culture holdout: "I try not to go into town very often. It is a mile just to the paved road." But the success of his Morningstar Tools bicycle tool company is gradually easing him into the mainstream.

Paul built his railbike "more as a work vehicle than for recreation." He used it years ago for checking timber harvest plans for various environmental organizations in Northern California along the upper headwaters of the Noyo river, from Willits to Fort Bragg.

Morningstar mostly rode tracks owned by logging interests where the rails could range from 50 to 68 mm

Photography by Paul Morningstar

Paul Morningstar designs and manufactures precision bicycle tools and hubs. (See Morningstar Tools in Appendix)

Photography by Paul Morningstar

Paul's design uses electrical conduit and a 12" front guide wheel.

wide. The distance between tracks could vary as much as 10 cm! So Paul's designs had to allow for these variables.

"My very first unit was two ten speeds side by side," he recalls. "After several attempts, we reached 100 meters but that was all. My buddy was not into the idea as much as me so I went solo."

"The welded outrigger wheel mount is about the most technical part," says Paul. "Mount it opposite your center of gravity. Spread the load out as far as possible when attaching to the bike."

While his railbike design is not what he considers remarkable, very little about Paul's experiences are common: "One particular day in a mild sleet storm at 630 meters elevation on a mountain pass, I endoed (flew end over end) myself, getting 'pitchpoled' over the bars, going uphill, luckily. I stepped on the handlebars going over

and found myself landing on a run. I stopped too soon and the flipping railbike continued forward, landing on top of me, knocking me to the railbed."

Bruised but undaunted, Paul quickly adds that he remembers other railbike experiences more fondly: "One New Year's day I was riding up to the summit through just enough snow to have it kick up off the front guides like ski tips in powder. The landscape was completely white except for the tops of the parallel brown rails. That day I

came from behind to within 25 feet of a bobcat. Closest I've ever gotten to one."

With his railbiking experiences ranging from breathtaking to life-threatening, Paul shares an ambition that seems common to all railbikers – a tendency to daydream about his next railbike design.

"A low unit with a sail would be the way to cross long, flat distances," Paul imagines. "Robert Storms from New

Photography by Paul Morningstar

The "Morningstar Railbike" folds up for travel off rail.

York sent me a photo of his recumbent unit," says Paul. "That's the way to go for my next rig, keeping the center of gravity the lower the better. 'Pitchpoling' over the bars once is enough!"

In closing our interview, Mr. Morningstar explained that he feels that railbiking is "one of the best kept secrets." Paul adds, "Most guys are pretty quiet about their experiences. I'm sure we think of our favorite tracks as we do our favorite trout pools."

Paul quickly contradicts his code of secrecy by inviting me to join him for a ride "next New Year's Day. We can do the whole 40 miles to Fort Bragg from Willits. It's so quiet you can hear the moon cruise by . . . There is an excellent Brewpub at the end."

Sign me up!

Photography by Paul Morningstar

A front view of Paul's bike.

MICHAEL FLORES
Leadville, Colorado

While you'd have to say that most railbikers have an odd side to them, Mr. Flores' lifestyle and railbike experiences seem particularly colorful. I was able to catch up with Mike between adventures as he was recuperating from a B.A.S.E. jumping accident in West Virginia wherein he suffered a broken back and two broken legs. I got the feeling that if it wasn't for his injuries, he wouldn't have stayed still long enough for an interview.

Between B.A.S.E. jumps Mike enjoys his street luge. What's a street luge? Picture a giant skateboard with skateboard wheels three times their normal size. Add some padding to lay on and glue some old tire tread on the bottom of your high-top sneakers for brakes. Hop on. Ride it down the steepest street you can find and hope for no cross traffic. What a rush!

Photography by Michael Flores

Mike Flores rests on a bench while pondering his next adventure.

Mike put his first luge together a couple of years before seeing some guy win the Extreme Games sailing down a hill on a land luge. Mr. Flores went on to explain that land lugeing is nowhere near as dangerous as when he jumped off the Golden Gate Bridge.

On June 30, 1991 Mike and a friend jumped off the north tower of the Golden Gate and parachuted to a waiting friend in a boat below. Also waiting, he discovered, was a Coast Guard cutter and the California Highway Patrol.

One night in jail and a promise not to parachute from the bridge ever again was the sentence.

Three weeks later, Flores and his pal again jumped off the Golden Gate. But true to his word, this time Mike used bungee chords – not a parachute.

Michael Flores also tells of diving for treasure 400 miles up the Rio Paragua river in Venezuela. His first trip diving at the site of a sunken Spanish galleon left him stranded in the jungle with a broken leg. I suggested that he stay home and watch these kinds of adventures on National Geographic's TV specials.

In his late 30's, Mike is single and has been a skydiver for 15 years. He was first introduced to railbiking by William Gillum and fell in love with the concept immediately. He dreams of a railbike trip on a line in Mexico through Copper Canyon that includes 39 bridges and 82 tunnels. He also mentioned the canyon features "an incredible rock face which I think is jumpable."

Flores has a fascination with "alternative modes" of transportation and has toyed with a number of railbike designs but, not surprisingly, has a special interest in adapting a wheelchair to rail travel. If successful with his rail-wheelchair, Michael can enjoy traveling the rails while recovering from his hard-earned injuries.

STEVE CRISE
Culver City, CA

About ten years ago Steve Crise happened to open an in-flight magazine to an article about something called a Railcycle. The article included an interview with the Railcycle's inventor, Richard Smart. Steve was fascinated by the story describing an activity which combined three of the things that he loves: history, railroading and exercise.

Shortly thereafter, Mr. Crise made a business trip to Idaho with his brother. Their trip included a visit with a man whose children happened to be patients of local dentist Richard Smart. A meeting was arranged.

As is his style, Smart went out of his way to share his Railcycle experience and took the Crise brothers for a ride on an abandoned rail line.

Steve was hooked!

Steve Crise glides through the desert.

Photography by Steve Lansing

Photography by Steve Lansing

Crise ponders crossing the railroad trestle in the distance. Note folded outrigger for off rail travel.

Upon returning home, Steve told all of his friends about the wonderful experience he had had riding the rails. He didn't have the money at the time to buy Smart's Railcycle, so he asked his friend, Steve Lansing to build three railbikes – one for himself, one for Steve Crise, and one for their mutual friend Dennis Bartlett.

They started with a basic Schwinn "beach cruiser" (no gears) and refined the design until they got something that worked and was reliable.

Once they settled on a design, Steve and his friend made three identical mountain bikes adapted for rail travel. These they rode extensively in Southern California, sometimes traveling right to the Mexican border.

But, Steve explains, "the problem with Southern California is that no matter how remote your location, there always seems to be some authority figure who will come out of nowhere and tell you to get off the tracks, even if they are abandoned.

Steve adds, however, "Fortunately we have been able to find a secret stretch of abandoned track that no one seems to know about." Yet.

Mr. Crise is a professional photographer and has shared some of his railbiking photographs in this book. He says that his wife is sympathetic with his railbriking interests, but never begs to ride along.

Like most railbikers, Steve Crise has a few experiences riding the rails which he remembers as special. The first of these was a spectacular crash wherein he sprained both thumbs after sailing over his handlebars onto the railbed. He had been gliding along when his front guide fell into a huge gap in the tracks and catapulted Steve and his bike into the air.

Steve also remembers when he and his friend Steve Lansing were in the middle of nowhere and Lansing's rear tire went flat. Visions of their bleached bones strewn across the railbed flashed

Photography by Steve Crise

I wish this picture were in color - we could join Crise in enjoying the deep blue desert sky and the brilliant white clouds.

through their minds. Fortunately, Lansing comes prepared for any eventuality and they made all the necessary repairs on the spot.

He remembers riding about 50 miles into the Mojave desert by Lone Pine near the Seral Mountains and coming to a stop because the tracks had been torn up. Steve explains, "Thieves tear up the rails to get to the ties. They load them onto trucks and drive them into Los Angeles to sell to nurseries for use in garden landscaping."

Steve Crise feels that the best thing about railbiking is meeting other people who have an interest in the sport, "There's so much to love about it. I like the people I meet railbiking, I can study the history of the various lines I ride and the places I visit, and I love to cycle." What more could you ask for?

———— O ————

Photography by Steve Crise

A disappointed Dennis considers the options. Thieves have removed the ties to sell to nurseries as landscape timbers.

RAILBIKE

STEVE LANSING
Long Beach, CA

Steve Lansing is pals with Steve Crise, whose story appears on the preceding pages. Mr. Lansing is married, with two children, and runs the Lansing Wheel Company, a manufacturer of gourmet go kart racing wheels.

Steve got his start in railbiking nine years ago when his friend Crise returned from his visit with Richard Smart in Idaho. Pictures of Smart's railbike got Mr. Lansing interested in making his own railbike and before long he had a one-speed Schwinn fitted with a guide and an outrigger and ready for testing.

Lansing's shop sits about 100 yards from the old Santa Ana Line of the Pacific Electric Railroad which operated in the 1920's and '30's. Steve admits a period of obsession over refining and debugging his railbike design. During this development process, Steve Crise served as chief advisor

Friend Dennis Bartlett (l.) and Steve Lansing (r.) pause at a crossing with Lansing's hand-made handcar.

Photography by Steve Crise

and senior guinea pig to flush out any design flaws.

Eventually, the two Steves got the bugs worked out and constructed two railbike systems attached to mountain bike frames. They were ready for adventure.

Lansing recalls, "Right before my son was born, I set off by myself on the old San Diego & Arizona Eastern Line which weaves its way in and out of Mexico. I experienced the solitude and beauty of the trip, took lots of pictures, and just had a wonderful time."

The two Steves then began taking overnight trips. They'd railbike one way the first day, stay overnight at a motel, and make the return trip the next day.

Lansing remembers that the bikes worked well on these trips, but that he was always a little uneasy about the prospect of the front guide jumping off the rail. He mentioned that because he

Photography by Steve Crise

Bartlett (l.) and Lansing (r.) discuss their progress. Steve Crise's railbike rests nearby.

did so much railbiking, he thinks maybe his technique was a little better than that of his friend Steve Crise and their mutual friend Dennis Bartlett who became the third member of their railbiking group.

On two separate trips one of Lansing partners suffered a derailment and crashed. He recalls that soon thereafter, he, too, had a rather serious crash, falling onto the railbed and hitting his head on the rail. "I was out for a few seconds," Steve explains, "and when I came to I was pretty shaken up. I didn't tell my wife about it for about a year or so, but from then on I always wore a helmet."

Steve's crash contributed to his new-found interest in riding a four-wheel handcar. "I figure they're a lot more stable and I'm less likely to crash," says Steve.

He hunted far and wide for a handcar, but came up empty. So he built one from scratch, without any plans.

Photography by Steve Crise

The handcar team of Bartlett and Lansing are dwarfed by the countryside they are traversing.

Once built, the handcar was ridden by Steve and Dennis, with Steve Crise riding along on his railbike. Lansing was now able to enjoy the ride a lot more. "I always wanted to relax on my railbike and enjoy the ride, but I found myself so focussed on the possibility of crashing, that I couldn't enjoy the scenery," says Lansing. "But once I built my handcar, all of that changed.

The railriding trio spent much of their time on the San Diego & Eastern Railroad running between Campo (outside San Diego) to El Centro, passing by Plaster City and through Carriso Gorge. The abandoned line traverses many large bridges and wound through several long tunnels.

Another favorite route was the rail line leading to a mining operation on Eagle Mountain. The line was in particularly good condition because it had only recently been abandoned by owner Kaiser Steel when it shut down its mine.

Lansing commented that "One thing that always discouraged me from

Lansing crossed this bridge when he came to it.

Photography by Steve Crise

doing more railbiking in the beginning was the possibility of getting caught." He shared Steve Crise's apprehension that someone would appear to tell him to get off of the tracks, even though they were clearly abandoned.

"It's getting better now, though," adds Steve, "It seems that people are accepting the sport more."

RAILBIKE

FRANCOISE & BERNARD MAGNOULOUX
Marly La Ville, France

"Bicycle Crusaders" is how the *HPV News* describes Françoise and Bernard Magnouloux. Their mission? To prove that you can go anywhere on a bicycle. That would include the town of Schefferville, Newfoundland, which didn't have even a dirt trail, let alone a road, leading to it.

I received a French fax from Bernard just as we were going to press on this book and he gave "an enthusiastic

Two flat tires were the result of this derailment.

YES" to my question of whether he would like to be included in our group of active railbikers. He had just returned from "a few days of cycling."

Bernard and Françoise have made many cycling expeditions, but none more exciting than their fishing party in Labrador, Newfoundland. The Magnouloux team encountered several bears scavenging through their campsites at night and suffered more than their share of equipment failures, including a double blowout after a spectacular derailment.

But the French team was up to the challenge and lived to share their experiences with us.

The Magnouloux tandem railbike resting en route.

Their railbike setup is unique. Not only is it a tandem railbike, the first I've seen, but its railbike outrigger cargo carrier doubles as a trailer for off rail travel.

Here you have the best of both worlds. Not only can you trailer all your camping gear to the tracks, but after some conversion adjustments, the whole thing will ride the rails. Plus, since it's a tandem, you can pretend to peddle and enjoy the ride while your partner does all the work. I want one.

Bernard has just published a booklet about railbikers (It's in French) and is anxious to share it. I haven't seen it yet, but if it contains anything like the railbike ingenuity and adventures Bernard has documented in the *HPV News*, his book will be well worth reading.

His "whereabouts:"

Françoise and Bernard Magnouloux
4 Chemin du Loup
F-95670 Marly La Ville, France

Photography by Bernard Magnouloux

The Magnouloux tandem railbike team.

RAILBIKE

RAILBIKING GUIDELINES

You need rails to go railbiking. The chapters of this book describe the skills required and dangers involved in railbiking. This information is not intended to discourage potential railbikers, but to present the realities involved in taking up the sport.

There are tens of thousands of legally abandoned rails in the United States alone. Locating abandoned rails near you is facilitated by several publications (See Appendix) and by contacting your local railroad company.

If you decide to railbike, ride safely and legally – follow these guidelines:

Guidelines

1. Ride only abandoned tracks.

2. Get permission from the right-of-way owner.

3. Respect the private property of surrounding areas.

4. Don't trespass in getting to and from the tracks.

This may seem like a prohibitive set of rules, but with an abundance of abandoned track available today, compliance with these guidelines is not difficult. So follow the guidelines above, and enjoy yourself.

———————— ○ ————————

Victor Vincente built this recumbent railbike.

Rail vehicle and creators Ned Levine & Dixon Newbold.

Courtesy of Lyllian Gillum

DESIGNING A RAILBIKE

You may want to skip this chapter if you don't really care about how a working railbike design can be developed. But if you'd like to know what goes into building a railbike and perhaps make design improvements of your own, you should probably read this chapter. It will give you a feel for the types of problems and design considerations that go into making a railbike that works.

As William Gillum pointed out, one of the questions that keeps coming up is "How do you provide a guidance system to keep the bike on the track?" Before discussing the mechanism for guiding the bike, it is important to understand some of the characteristics of the track itself.

First of all, not all tracks are the same. They differ in size, shape, weight, separation, surface width, etc. Different countries use different types

If you are going to build a railbike, it's important to have a workshop and a big sign that says so.

# RAILBIKE

International Track Guages

3 ft 3½ inches (1,000 mm)
East Africa, India, Malaysia
Chile, and Argentina

3 ft 6 inches (1,067 mm)
Japan, Australia, Sudan,
West Africa, New Zealand

4 ft 8½ inches (1,435 mm)
United States, Canada, China
Egypt, Turkey, Iran, Japan,
Peru, Britain, Europe, Brazil,
Australia, and Mexico

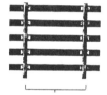

5 ft 0 inches (1,524 mm)
Russia, Spain, Portugal,
and Finland

5 ft 3 inches (1,600 mm)
Ireland, Australia and Brazil

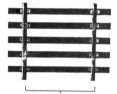

5 ft 6 inches (1,676 mm)
India, Pakistan, and
Argentina

of track. So it's important that your railbike can adjust to these variables if you plan to railbike around the world.

Not only are tracks manufactured differently, but climatic conditions can also change the tracks. On Saturday, July 15, 1995, the associated press reported 16 of 53 train cars derailing in Athens, Ohio because high temperatures caused the track to shift 14 inches. As rails heat up, they expand and move.

So not only does a working design have to work on the tracks on which you test it, it also has to be able to accommodate changes in the tracks themselves.

What follows is a chronicle of trial and error tests of various designs which ultimately evolved into a working railbike. My goal was to build something from "off-the-shelf" components available at any hardware store, for under $100. The finished product is nothing fancy and certainly not the best design available (See Appendix). But it is inexpensive, durable, portable, easy to assemble, and it works.

Over the past 100 years, there have been scores of railbike designs and adaptations, most of which probably work pretty well. In building my own railbike, I wanted to understand why there had been so many variations on a product which seemed to be fairly simple.

My goal was to develop an attachment for a bicycle which would allow the user to ride to the tracks while carrying the attachment kit, assemble and attach it to the bicycle, and ride on the rails. I also wanted the attachment to be simple to assemble and to be safe for the rider should the bike somehow come off of the tracks.

Rather than simply taking a design I knew would work and adapting it to my personal preferences, I chose to try

All rails are not the same.

Son Joe and daughter Haley join Dad on an adventure.

to start from scratch and learn more by doing it the hard way.

This chapter summarizes the evolutionary design process I went through to arrive at what I feel is an acceptable product. I have numbered each of the different designs as I went along so I could keep track of what I was doing. As I review the designs, I will share the lessons I learned, some which seem obvious, and the considerations that were part of the development process. The design I ultimately arrived at is certainly not the best ever, nor has its evolution been completed. But it is a design that works well and is fairly easy to build, and one which you may wish to build yourself as a "starter railbike."

In the Beginning - The X-1

Twenty five years ago I built what I called a railbike. It was slow, heavy, impractical and there were other things wrong with it that I can't remember. But it worked, and it was a fun project, and I couldn't write this book without including a little information about it.

So I started this chronicle of my railbike development process by rebuilding my original railbike to add a sense of history and depth to my work.

Since this was my first railbike design, I refer to it as the X-1. It was essentially a rectangular platform with four wheels, two on each track. A bicycle frame was mounted in the center with passenger seats on each side. The rear axle was driven by the three speed bicycle. (Plans for the X-1 are available - see Order Form)

I removed the wheel and spokes from the rear hub and mounted a 14" v-belt pulley onto the hub flange, using the holes that had been used for the spokes.

As an option, you may simply remove the tire and tube from the rear wheel of the bicycle and use the rim as a pulley. This requires a more precise belt length, but it works.

The rear axle was a length of ½-inch iron pipe with a 5-inch pulley in the center and standard plumbing flanges at each end. I put bolts through the solid rubber wheels and through slightly larger discs of sheet steel and bolted both to the pipe flanges.

For the test run of the recreated X-1, I once again was able to drag my family along, this time it was my own children who provided the complaints. The day was too hot, the kids had better things to do, and the tracks were more overgrown than I remembered.

Also, the tunnel leading to the next town was boarded up and the trestle which spanned our nearby waterway had been locked in a permanent "up" position. To further demonstrate the lack of respect given to abandoned railroads, someone had put a parking lot, complete with cyclone fencing, right over one end of the tracks.

But about a mile of open track still remained and that's all we would need to test the X-1.

Not much to look at but the X-1 is lots of fun.

At this point I should add that throughout my railbike development process, I had asked my children not to tell anyone about what I was doing. There weren't any "No Trespassing" signs and with both ends of the tracks blocked, I knew I didn't have to worry about oncoming trains. Yet it was in a residential area and I felt someone would find a reason to stop me if they found out.

"Don't worry dad, we won't tell anybody. Especially not any of our friends," was the reply from both teenage daughter and son. At first I was proud of the loyalty they expressed in respecting my request for secrecy. Only later did they admit that my secret was safe with them only because they feared being humiliated in the eyes of their peers for having a father who plays with railbikes.

I suppose I couldn't blame them, but I was crushed. But I knew my secret was safe, even though my ego was taking a beating.

So, under a veil of secrecy, we assembled the X-1 one Saturday morning, and hopped aboard.

I figure our total weight was close to 600 pounds including railbike, my two passengers and myself. The bicycle I used for power had a three speed gear reduction inside the rear hub so I started off in low gear.

As I started to peddle, the drive belt from the bicycle to the rear axle slipped a little since I bought one an inch too large. But we moved forward and steadily picked up speed.

Soon I was able to shift into second gear, and then third, as we whisked down the tracks. The X-1 ran like a champ and in no time we were approaching the cyclone fence at the end of the line. Fortunately, the X-1 came with a effective braking system.

On command, each passenger pulled back on a pivoting length of lead pipe whose other end rubbed gratingly

Fred Flintstone designed the handbrakes for the X-1.

against the track surface, bringing us to an obnoxiously noisy, but controlled stop.

The X-1 was a success! I was delighted!

"Now can we go home?" The passengers asked. I knew the significance of the moment was lost on the young, and I forgave them for not being overwhelmed. So after recording the moment on 3 or 4 rolls of film, we packed up and left.

THE X-2

Though the X-1 was a success, it was not the portable, single-rider railbike I was interested in.

I wanted something anyone could assemble and enjoy and attach to their present bicycle. So I started my design process as simply as possible: A single bike, on a single track.

The only trick, I felt, was to keep the bike on the track.

The X-2 was an attempt at a single rail balancing act.

So I built the X-2 with two sets of guides, one set to keep the front wheel on track, and one set to keep the back wheel on track.

The guides were skateboard wheels, mounted on a vertical axis on each side of the track, and extending about 3/4-inch below the top of the track. The guides were aligned by supports anchored to the axles of each bicycle wheel.

This design seemed to be what I wanted: Very simple.

But the simplicity of this designed proved also to be it biggest fault. The skateboard wheels, with their near frictionless operation, worked very well. But keeping the front bicycle wheel on track was almost impossible. Since the front guides were mounted behind the front wheel, it tended to steer to one side or the other and the next thing I knew I was bouncing along on the railroad ties.

This was especially true when riding on rails whose surface had been slanted inward from the tremendous

Guide wheels in front of the rear bicycle wheel were designed to keep it on track.

weight and wear of passing trains over the years. The profile of the typical train wheel shows why it tends to wear down the inside edge of the tracks. The wheels only have one guide flange which presses against the inside edge of each track, ultimately wearing them down on that side.

Trying to ride a bicycle on a 3-inch wide track is hard enough, but keeping it on a 3-inch track that is slanted is even more difficult. The front wheel keeps wanting to turn inward between the two tracks.

The solution? Put another set of guide wheels <u>in front</u> of the front bicycle wheel.

The X-3

I had initially avoided putting a fixed set of guide wheels in front of the bicycle because of concern for obstacles or irregularities which might be on the track. I figured that if I was going to run into something, it would be best to hit it first with the 26" bicycle wheel than with a rigidly attached set of small guide wheels.

I tend to overbuild — the angle iron used on the X-2 and X-3 added about 100 pounds. I should have used titanium.

Here's an example of stuff attached to the sides of rails that can get in the way of railbike guidance systems.

But it was clear from the X-2 experience that additional guidance was needed, so a forward set of guide wheels was added.

Here I should mention another feature of common railroad tracks which tends to limit design possibilities. This feature I can best describe as an unfortunately shallow clearance along both sides of each track, which limits the depth that any guidance system can extend below the rail surface.

A seemingly countless array of bolts, wires, welds, boards, plates, and other construction accessories are attached to the sides of railroad tracks. Each has a purpose, some known only to those who laid the track. But each is a potential roadblock to any guidance system that protrudes too deeply along the side of the rail.

Since the guidance system for trains uses only the inside of each track, the preponderance of blocking attachments occur on the outside of the tracks. But for practical purposes, you may assume that you can enjoy only about 3/4" of clearance along the upper edges of each track.

For this reason, the guides on all of my test designs only extended this 3/4" along the sides of the track.

So the X-3 had a pair of guide wheels at three points: one set each in

The X-3 had an extra set of guide wheels.

front and behind the front bicycle wheel, and one set in front of the rear bicycle wheel. I figured that this would certainly keep the front wheel of the bicycle from coming off of the track.

And I was right. In testing the X-3 I found that in fact both wheels of the bicycle hugged the track just as I had hoped.

But I also re-learned a lesson from my youth which is one of the fundamental principles of riding a bicycle: When you start to tip over to one side, you need to turn the front wheel in that direction to keep from falling over.

Well, since I was successful at keeping the front wheel aligned with the track, I was unable to steer it to keep from tipping over. So I tipped over. Again and again.

Back to the drawing board.

Re-learning the basic principle of how to balance a bicycle was an humbling experience. I felt a little better months later when I learned that none other than William J. Gillum himself had made the same design mistake on his first railbike, 20 years ago.

The X-4

I suppose I knew all along that my railbike would need an "outrigger" support like all the other examples I had seen while researching the subject. But I had wanted to experience first hand why a single rail design wouldn't work, and now I understood.

Actually, the X-3 would have worked if I could have kept my balance. All I needed was one of those long balance poles that tightrope walkers use in the circus.

So I started work on the X-4 which would have an outrigger support resting on the other track. The design was

An outrigger helps. The X-4 worked well but was vulnerable to debris and derailments.

similar to that of Mr. Gillum which appeared in Popular Mechanics. I tried to improve on his design by spring loading the outrigger guide wheels to allow for variations in distance between the tracks.

Like Mr. Gillum's design, the X-4 had a guide wheel mounted to ride on the inside of the track just below each

Spring-loaded dual wheels on the outrigger.

of the bicycle wheels. The axles for these guide wheels were adjustable both vertically and obliquely from the track to provide the proper depth and angle of contact with the track.

For simplicity, I made the outrigger out of a single length of steel tubing instead of the various plumbing fittings Mr. Gillum had used. The outrigger was attached to the bicycle wheel axles using screw-on "pegs" frequently used by cyclists who perform bicycle tricks.

Testing the X-4 was a pleasure. It worked well. The guide wheels kept the bicycle on track and the spring-loaded outrigger wheels provided the balance and support needed to keep from tipping over.

Adjustable guides along the inside of the rail.

I had succeeded, with help from Mr. Gillum's design, in building a single rider railbike that worked. I was happy about that.

But there was a problem with this design which made it less durable than I had hoped. The guide wheels which rode inside the track adjacent to the bicycle wheels were vulnerable to damage should they encounter an obstacle or if the bicycle were to somehow come off the track. I wanted a design that would allow for what I feel is inevitable - the unexpected.

The X-5

About this time in my research and development process, my son Joe got sick and had to stay home from school

The X-5 was my first model to use an extended front guide (good idea). Bent conduit was used for the outrigger.

one day. Good father that I am, I did what had to be done to make him well. I went to the video store to rent a movie for him to watch.

I happened to pick up a family adventure film, called "The Quest," with a modern-day Tom Sawyer on the cover. I flipped the box over to read the storyline summary and was surprised to see a picture of the hero tooling along on his homemade railbike.

I'm not sure Joe ever got to watch the movie, but I studied the railbike

scenes over and over. The "Quest design" had some features I had not seen before. A single guide for the front wheel extended well in front of the bicycle, as suggested in the 1908 Sears & Roebuck advertisement. The guide appeared to "lock" onto each side of the track with flat steel tabs pressing against the sides of the track.

The front guide was also "hinged" so it could bounce up if it encountered obstacles, and the whole front guide system could be lifted up and fastened to the handle bars without detaching it.

The hinged front guide houses two skateboard wheels which ride on top of the rail.

A single roller supports the outrigger.

This would allow a rider to ride to and from the tracks with the front guide lifted up and out of the way, but still attached to the front wheel. I liked that.

Guidance for the rear bicycle wheel was simple. There wasn't any. Somehow, the rear bicycle wheel stayed aligned and on track without any separate guidance apparatus.

The outrigger design was also simple. It consisted of a triangular support attached just below the handlebars and at the rear axle, and extending to a single roller on the opposite track at right angles with the rear bicycle axle. The roller had no flanges to keep it centered on the supporting track.

With some modifications, this design was the model for the X-5. Unlike the Quest design, I attached the front outrigger support to the front bicycle wheel axle instead of to the handle bar neck. I did this in the interest of time since I already had the attachment fittings from the X-4.

This proved to be a mistake since the center of gravity on any bike, including railbikes, is so high. This puts tremendous pressure on the outrigger attachment points if they are located too low on the bicycle, such as at the axle bolts. I suspected this was to be a weakness.

But the testing of the X-5 was wonderful. The front wheel guide worked well, even when I deliberately ran it into some rubble. The rear wheel stayed on track as it had in the movie, and the whole experience was a plus. I was making progress.

The X-6

I moved the point of attachment for the front outrigger support up to the neck of the bicycle's handlebars. I lowered the rear outrigger attachment

to below the rear axle. This greatly improved stability and balance.

For the first time I used two diameters of electrical conduit (3/4" and 1¼") for the outrigger arms so they could telescope and collapse for transport and storage.

The telescoping adjustment is very low tech but very effective. Cut six 4" slits at the end of the outer 1¼" conduit. Slide the 3/4" conduit inside and close up the slits with a hose clamp. Very strong, very secure.

Some of the 1¼" plumbing fixtures used to mount the roller at the end of the outrigger were left only hand-tightened to allow some flexibility.

This design was yet another improvement and worked well, but I wanted to try a different type of outrigger roller to see what guidance improvements might be possible.

The X-6 was the first "X" model to use an adjustable telescoping outrigger.

Test driver Joe Mellin signals that the new X-7 design is safe for dad to try.

The X-7

I made two "improvements" to create this model. One was a good idea, the other was not.

First, I provided additional bracing to the outrigger's attachment at the rear axle. I used angle iron to brace the horizontal outrigger both perpendicular and parallel to the bike. This improved stability a lot.

I also replaced the outrigger roller with three wheels, the middle of which had a one inch smaller diameter. The larger wheels were spaced to fit along each side of the track to "grip" it.

Bad idea.

Though the wheels added more counterbalancing weight to the bike, they were heavy and just that much more to carry to and from the tracks. There was no perceivable improvement in performance. The outrigger did not "grip" the rail as I had hoped.

A simple roller at the end of the outrigger is all that is needed. Its function is simply to support the bike, not to help steer it.

A roller is all you need.

Designed to "grip" the rail. Bad idea.

As with the X-6, the X-7 and all future models included a cargo basket fastened to the outrigger. This helps balance the bike and carries useful stuff. I always carry my tools, camera, lunch and an inflatable liferaft when crossing bridges.

The X-8

Though this trial and error design refinement process could go on indefinitely, the X-8 is as far as we'll go in this book.

The X-8 uses a roller on the outrigger and has an optional configuration to allow more clearance above the railbed. On the X-6 and X-7 the hori-

Not an engineering marvel, but the X-8 is cheap, durable, and it works.

zontal outrigger pole was only about a foot above the rail ties which was a problem in tall weeds.

By swinging the angle iron brace back and up behind the rear axle, and adding a vertical extension to the roller mount, clearance can be increased to about two feet.

The front guide on the X-8 stayed the same as on prior models since it works well.

The X-8 design, while not an engineering marvel, meets the goals I had set at the outset. It was built with "off-the-shelf" materials for under $100 and is simple to assemble and very durable.

Plans for the X-8 are available (See Order Form). The design of the X-8 is not as advanced as, for example, Richard Smart's Railcycle (Plans available - See Appendix) which is a better choice for the serious railbiker.

Whichever model or design you choose, building a railbike is an enjoyable project which leads to an even more enjoyable sport.

DO-IT-YOURSELF

Railbikes are currently not mass produced and are not available commercially. Many railbikers feel that this is the way it should be.

The inconvenience of having to build your own railbike tends to weed out the casual rider who might have neither the skills nor disposition to approach the sport safely and responsibly. Several of the railbikers interviewed in this book suggest that "if you want a railbike, build your own." It will make you understand the skills required and dangers involved.

If you decide you want to build your own railbike, several options are available ranging from designing your own to using plans for a proven model (See Appendix). Many "first-timers" do a little of both. Everyone seems to make their own "improvements."

In building your own railbike, you should start with the right bicycle.

Joe Mellin cruises past the railbike pickup truck.

While using a bike with narrow racing or touring tires might work for you, using a bike with wider tires, like the old balloon or mountain bike tires, is probably a better idea. Wider tires will provide better traction and a greater margin for alignment error than thin tires.

It isn't necessary to use a bike with a lot of gearing options since, by their nature, railroads don't have any steep grades. While a bike with at least three speeds is ideal, an old single speed, coaster brake, balloon-tired cruiser will work well. A modern mountain or street bike with fifteen or more speeds is an overkill in terms of gearing options, but may be preferable for traveling to and from the tracks.

Brakes are important. And this includes a parking brake of some sort.

You'll want to be able to stop after going forward. But equally important is the ability to keep your railbike from rolling backward on an incline. Railbike guidance designs typically are built to guide forward travel. If the bike rolls backward, it will usually derail and this is not good. So if you are stopping on an incline, make sure to use some sort of tire block or clamp to prevent rollback.

This book is not intended as a guide to building a railbike, rather it is meant to expose the reader to the many issues to be considered in railbike design and construction. Building a railbike is a challenging project. Creating the finished project can be a wonderful experience, and the safe, legal use of a homemade railbike on abandoned rails is truly a joy.

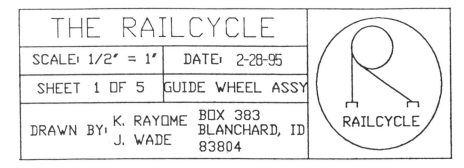

Here's the signature block do-it-yourselfers will find on each of 12 pages of blueprints for Richard Smart's Railcycle.

RAILBIKE

BIBLIOGRAPHY

Rail Riders, Ron Forster, River Bend Mill, Franklin, NH, 1982.

Right-Of-Way – Guide to Abandoned Railroads in the United States, Third Edition, Maverick Publications, 1992.

American Railbike Association Handbook, by W. Gillum, 1977.

Sears & Roebuck Catalog, 1908 edition.

That Was Railroading, George B. Adbill, Superior Publishing Company, 1958.

Pedal Power, by James C. McCullagh, Rodale Press, 1968.

500 Great Rail Trails, J.A. Winterich, K. Ryan, Living Planet Press, Washington, DC, 1994.

Human Powered Vehicle News (HPV News),, Monthly Newsletter of the International Human Powered Vehicle Association.

The Historical Guide to North American Railroads, Compiled by George H. Drury, Kalmbach Publishing Co., Milwaukee, WI, 1985. History of 160 railroads abandoned since 1930.

O & W, by William F. Helmer, Howell-North, Berkeley, CA, 1959. History of the New York, Ontario & Western Railway, abandoned in its entirety in 1957.

The Electric Interurban Railways in America, by George W. Hilton & John F. Due, Stanford University Press, Stanford, CA, 1964. 16,000 miles of the U.S. interurban railway system, virtually all abandoned, are described and mapped.

BIBLIOGRAPHY

Tracking Ghost Railroads in Colorado, by Robert Ormes, Century One Press, Colorado Springs, CO, 1975.

Ghost Railroads of Tennessee, by Elmer G. Sulzer, V.A. Jones, Indianapolis, IN, 1975.

Availability and Reuse of Abandoned Railroad Rights-of-Way, based on the Harbridge House Study, U.S. Department of Transportation, Washington, D.C., 1977.

Benefit Estimates for Recreational Re-Use of Abandoned Railroad Rights-of-Way, Institute of Urban and Regional Research, University of Iowa, Iowa City, IA, 1975.

Ces Silencieuses Petites Machines, by Florian Grenier, Quebec, Canada, 1990.

Anybody's Bike Book, by Tom Cuthbertson, Ten Speed Press, Berkeley, CA, 1979.

Recreational Reuse of Abandoned Railroad Rights-of-Way: A Bibliography and Technical Resource Guide for Planners, by G. P. Ames, Council of Planning Librarians, Chicago, IL, 1981.

Rights of Way for Recreation - Outdoor Recreation Action Report #25, Bureau of Outdoor Recreation, Wash. DC, 1972.

A Guide to Hassle-Free Railroad Right-of-Way Conversion by Stuart H. Macdonald, Parks & Recreation, April, 1980.

Handy Railroad Atlas, by Rand McNally, Chicago, IL, published every 2 to 3 years.

———————— o ————————

RAILBIKE

APPENDIX

Information Resources:

RAILBIKE INTERNATIONAL, Newsletter, networking contacts, research support. $16./yr. 11 Library Place, San Anselmo, CA 94960 – FAX: 415-453-8888,
E-mail: RAILBIKES @ AOL.COM

RAILBIKE EXPRESS, Newsletter, $22./yr. Peter Alexander, Box 73787, Kowloon Central Post Office, Hong Kong.

RIGHT-OF-WAY – Guide to Abandoned Railroads, Valuable reference for locating abandoned railroads. $20. c/o Balboa Publishing, 11 Library Place, San Anselmo, CA 94960.

HUMAN POWERED VEHICLE NEWS, Exceptional source of information on railbike development. Membership & newsletter, $25./yr. IHPVA, Box 51255, Indianapolis, IN 46251-0255, (708) 742-4933.

AMERICAN RAILROAD ASSOCIATION, Railroad Companies' information clearinghouse, policies and positions.
50 F Street, N.W., Washington, D.C. 20001.

AMERICAN RAILBIKE ASSOCIATION HANDBOOK, William Gillum's original information handbook includes plans for tandem railbike. $10. c/o Balboa Publishing, 11 Library Place, San Anselmo, CA, 94960.

RAIL RIDERS, Ron Forster's overview of railbike development over the years including the development of his lightweight rail wheels and "RON'S RIDER" vehicle. $12. c/o Balboa Publishing, 11 Library Place, San Anselmo, CA 94960.

RAILS-TO-TRAILS CONSERVANCY, Conversion of abandoned railroad rights-of-way to recreational use. 1400 Sixteenth Street, N.W., Suite 300, Washington, D.C. 20036.

CALIFORNIA STATE RAILROAD MUSEUM LIBRARY, 113 "I" Street, Sacramento, CA 95814. (916) 323-8073.

PATENT LIBRARY, Patent copies and research provided by fax and/or mail. City of Sunnyvale Library, 1500 Partridge Avenue, Bldg. #7, Sunnyvale, CA 408-730-7489.

PORT OF TILLAMOOK BAY, 400 Blimp Boulevard, Tillamook, OR, 97141. (503) 842-2413.

CES SILENCIEUSES PETITES MACHINES, french railbike book by Florian Grenier, CP 128 Sullivan, Quebec, Canada J0Y 2N0. 250 pages - $22.

——————————— **Plans & Parts** ———————————

RAILCYCLE PLANS, $85. Patented by Richard Smart, 3502 Buckskin Road, Coeur d'Alene, ID 83814.

CERAMIC MAGNETS FOR RAILCYCLE, $45. plus $5. shpg, Coati Express, 1006 Frederick Street, S.E., Olympia, WA 98501-1930. (360) 357-5405, E-mail: BWANO @ AOL.COM

MODEL X-1 & MODEL X-8 PLANS, $10. for each model. Balboa Publishing, 11 Library Place, San Anselmo, CA 94960.

RAIL RIDERS & WHEELS by Ron Forster, Rail Riders, ' ATTN: Ron Forster, Box 249, Antrim, NH 03440.

RAILBIKE PLANS, $20. order/info. from Richard Bentley, Mount Arab, Box 786, Tupper Lake, NY 12986.

RAILBIKE

──── RAILBIKE TRIP LOG ────

Name: Ann & Michael Rohde

Date: August 14, 1995

Riders in Party: 2

Start Point: Garibaldi

End Point: Jetty

Route (stations/towns): Barview, Ocean Lake, Saltair, Rockaway, Maddon

Total miles: 18.4 round trip

Travel time: about 3 hours with stop for lunch

Track conditions: clear, level

Points of Interest: ocean beach, sea stacks

Comments: Great afternoon ride.

──── Sketch of Route ────

Jetty

To Tillamook →

Rockaway

Garibaldi
Barview

Pacific Ocean

Tillamook Bay

This Railbike Trip Log form is provided so you may keep a record of your railbike adventures. Balboa Publishing grants permission for the owner of this book to reproduce this form if additional copies are needed. Or, if you prefer, additional copies of this form may be obtained by purchasing additional copies of this book.

——— RAILBIKE TRIP LOG ———

Name:

Date:

Riders in Party:

Start Point:

End Point:

Route (stations/towns):

Total miles:

Travel time:

Track conditions:

Points of Interest:

Comments:

——Sketch of Route——————————————————————————

RAILBIKE T-Shirt

The colorful RAILBIKE Logo T-Shirt features a traveling railbiker on the front, and a railroad semaphore on the back — its horizontal arm and red light give the universal "STOP" signal to anyone who may be coming up behind you.   This shirt is a must for any serious railbiker. $18.00.

ORDER FORM

 PHONE ORDERS
415-453-8886
Mon-Fri 8am-4pm

 FAX ORDERS
415-453-8888
24 hours a day

 MAIL ORDERS
11 Library Place
San Anselmo
CA 94960

Item#		Quantity	Cost	Amount
700	Railbike International annual membership		$16.00	
701	"RAILBIKE — Cycling On Abandoned Railroads"		16.95	
702	"RIGHT-OF-WAY — A Guide to Abandoned Railroads"		19.95	
703	RAILBIKE T-shirt (M, L, XL, XXL)		18.00	
704	Plans for Railbike X-1		10.00	
705	Plans for Railbike X-8		10.00	
706	"RAIL RIDERS" book by Ron Forster		12.00	
707	"AMERICAN RAILBIKE ASSOCIATION" handbook		10.00	

—— SHIPPING CHARGES: —— First item $3.00 Two items $5.00 Additional items $1.00 each	CA Res. add Sales Tax	
	Shipping	
	TOTAL	

METHOD OF PAYMENT: □ CHECK (make payable to BALBOA PUBLISHING)

□ Mastercard or Visa CARD # _____ expires ___ / ___

SHIP TO:

Name _____

Street _____

City _____ St _____ Zip _____

Telephone _(_____)_____

——BALBOA PUBLISHING CORPORATION, 11 LIBRARY PLACE, SAN ANSELMO, CA 94960——

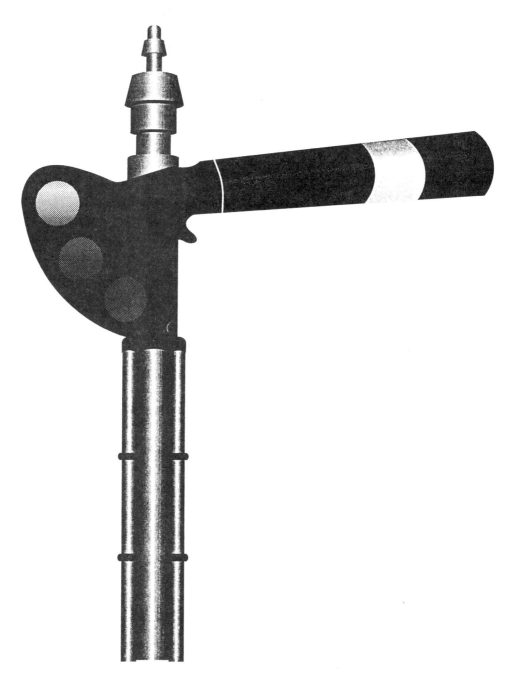

Balboa Publishing, 11 Library Place, San Anselmo, CA 94960 • BALBOAPUB @ AOL . COM